GHOST
STORIES
of
OHIO

Edrick Thay

GHOST
HOUSE

Ghost House Books

The Publisher: Ghost House Books
Distributed by Lone Pine Publishing
10145 – 81 Avenue
Edmonton, AB T6E 1W9
Canada
Website: http://www.ghostbooks.net

National Library of Canada Cataloguing in Publication Data

Thay, Edrick, 1977–
    Ghost stories of Ohio
    ISBN 1–894877–09–8
    1. Ghosts—Ohio. 2. Legends—Ohio. I. Title.
GR110.O48T42 2002   398.2'0977105   C2002-910731-8

Editorial Director: Nancy Foulds
Project Editors: Shelagh Kubish, Chris Wrangler
Illustrations Coordinator: Carol Woo
Production Coordinator: Jennifer Fafard
Cover Design: Gerry Dotto
Layout & Production: Lynett McKell, Jeff Fedorkiw
Photo Credits: Every effort has been made to accurately credit photographers. Any errors
or omissions should be directed to the publisher for changes in future editions. The photographs and illustrations in this book are reproduced with the kind permission of the
following sources: Library of Congress (p. 3, 9: HABS, OHIO, 79–ZOAR, 3–2; p. 4–5, 43,
127: HABS, OHIO, 79–ZOAR, 2–1; p. 15: USW3–0298–84–E; p. 26, 146: HAER, OHIO,
31–LOVE.V, 1–1; p. 56: USZ62–112049; p. 91, 119: HABS, OHIO, 31–CINT, 5–2 Nitrate;
p. 114: HABS, NEV, 15–VIRG, 35–4; p. 129: HABS, OHIO, 79–ZOAR, 2–4; p. 131: HABS,
OHIO, 79–ZOAR, 16–1; p. 143: USF33–003490–M3); Douglas C. Meyers, Wooster, Ohio
(p. 20); Ohio Historical Society (p. 32: 11629); Fairport Harbor Historical Society (p. 37);
Kevin Furniss (p. 73); Victoria Theatre (p. 81: Andy Snow); Donald L. Barnett (p. 98, 109);
Glenbow Archives (p. 116: NA–2059–5); The Knights of the Golden Trail of the Loveland
Castle (p. 138); David Cater, Noble County, www.noblecountyohio.com (p. 167); Rebecca
S. Shott, Parahaunt (p. 169, 186, 189); Sandusky Library (p. 172: JOIS–018; p. 174: JOIS–103);
Edrick Thay (p. 39, 53, 65, 68, 77).

The stories, folklore and legends in this book are based on the author's collection of
sources including individuals whose experiences have led them to believe they have
encountered phenomena of some kind or another. They are meant to entertain, and neither
the publisher nor the author claims these stories represent fact.

We acknowledge the financial support of the Government of Canada through the Book
Publishing Industry Development Program (BPIDP) for our publishing activities.

PC: P5

Dedication

To the McInturf family of New Richmond, Ohio—you have my love and you will always be close to my heart. Thank you for everything you have given me. To my deepest regret, I'll never be able to repay the debt.

Contents

Acknowledgments

Many thanks go out to those who stoke the storytelling tradi-tion—those who have investigated the unexplained and have worked to bring the stories out from the shadows. Thank you to Ohio writers Connie Cartmell, Chris Woodyard and Richard Crawford, who provided me with excellent advice and leads. Without their curiosities, this book would have suffered.

My deepest gratitude also goes to the many people who allowed me to interview them or provided me with informa-tion. For your help you have my thanks: Carol Bertone of the Fairport Harbor Lighthouse and Museum, Kay Bork at the Granville Public Library, Tamar Chute of the Ohio State University Archives, Pamela Faust at the Thurber House, Eddie Fox, Tina Harrah of the Ohio Historical Society, researcher Andrew Henderson, Karen Jones from Ohio University, Tammy Muente at the Taft Museum of Art, Robert Murnan of the Cleveland Research Center, Doug Myers of Wooster Fire Station Number 1, Audrey Orr of the Buxton Inn, Ann Pilarczyk, researcher Bill Samuels and researcher Jeff Schmidt.

The in-house staff at Ghost House provided constant sup-port and invaluable advice throughout the writing of this book, but the writing is just one small step in the creation of a book. For their editing, Chris Wangler and Shelagh Kubish have my gratitude. Without you, *Ghost Stories of Ohio* would be a lesser book. For her talent at obtaining the images that breathe life into our text, Carol Woo has my deepest appreci-ation. And for their work in crafting the book's presentation, Lynett McKell and Jeff Fedorkiw have my thanks.

Finally, I would like to thank Nancy Foulds and Shane Kennedy, whose faith and support throughout this project have been unwavering and invaluable.

Introduction

I welcomed the opportunity to write this book of Ohio ghost stories. It was a homecoming of sorts; I'd spent a great deal of time in Columbus and Cincinnati and embraced the chance to learn more about the seventeenth American state, where the South, Midwest and Northeast converge. Ohio straddles the steel factories of Pennsylvania, the coal mines of West Virginia and Kentucky, the automotive plants of Michigan and the fields of Indiana. The state has produced seven American presidents, among them Civil War General Ulysses S. Grant, James A. Garfield and William McKinley.

Researching ghost stories gave me a chance to see a different side of the state's history—a history not of dates and names, but of people and places, of those who've contributed to the character of Ohio. Ohio's personality is boisterous, open and warm; she can be cosmopolitan, rustic or a combination of both. They're qualities that come through warmly, like the rays of the sun, in folklore and story. When Ohio celebrates its bicentennial in 2003, its citizens will no doubt take time to reflect on the past. That's what I hope these ghost stories do—I hope they help to celebrate the past.

Of course, ghost stories are not for everyone. Skeptics will always question whether or not ghosts exist, while ghost hunters will never doubt their existence. This book is not written for paranormal fanatics or paranormal skeptics; it is written for the Ohioan—for anyone who has an interest in perusing an album of snapshots that captures life throughout the state as it has grown. It's a chance to see again a world that we often take for granted: the world around us. As much as these stories are about the strange and unusual, they are also about the Buckeye State.

It's been almost a year since I was last in Ohio, and while the time I spent there was relatively brief, something about the place got under my skin. It was familiar, yet exotic—the combination has since insinuated itself in places reserved for only the fondest of memories. Everyone I met greeted me as if I was already a friend, as if the word stranger did not exist. Many of these people I still consider my friends; others I even consider family. I look forward to returning soon, but until I do, I will have to content myself with revisiting my memories and cherishing my work on this book.

I don't have any grand expectations for this collection. I hope it allows Ohioans to experience the familiar in a whole new way and all others to become familiar with one of America's most fascinating states. If the book fails in this regard, then I hope, at the very least, that these stories are entertaining and informative, as the best stories should be.

1
Paranormal
Legends

~

Every state has its own legends. Like heirlooms, they are unique treasures passed down from generation to generation. This transmission continues an oral tradition that seems to lose currency with each passing day in our information culture. In the past, families congregated around the fireplace to tell stories, but today they sit in silence, huddled around a television screen. The value of legends cannot be underestimated. They connect us with our pasts and to times that might exist only in imagination or memory. To listen to them is to experience histories not recognized or acknowledged by the official record. It is to experience something completely different.

~

The Mothman

People have called it a weather balloon. One man thought it was a creature fallen from the moon, curious to visit the planet that had sent so many satellites to its home. Another man went so far as to claim that the creature was nothing more than his mother-in-law. Even a county sheriff joined in the speculation, certain that it was just a member of the heron family. Mrs. Mallette, one of the first to spot the infamous creature in 1966, told Roger Bennett of the *Athens Messenger* that she hoped others would see it, and that when they did, "it [would scare] them as much as it did us. Maybe then they'll believe the thing exists and we're not dreaming."

Nobody knows for certain what two young couples saw while out for a drive one fall evening. Regardless, word of the mysterious creature roaming the land soon spread through southeastern Ohio and West Virginia—accounts newsworthy enough to merit attention in the *New York Times* and in the Saigon edition of *Stars and Stripes*. The couples, the Mallettes and Scarberrys, were out on what was then a series of roads criss-crossing through the McClintic Wildlife Sanctuary, near Point Pleasant, West Virginia, just across the Ohio state border. The setting was eerie enough: government-owned property near an old abandoned TNT factory that had long ago yielded to the ravages of time.

The Mallettes and the Scarberrys slowed their car as they approached a rise in the road. They noticed that their progress up the road was not going unnoticed. There, in the bushes, the two couples saw what they could only describe as a set of glowing red eyes, set six inches apart. Shaken, they continued on, only to encounter the creature again when they finally reached the paved road back to civilization.

But instead of seeing only its eyes, the couples saw the creature in its entirety—a towering human-like being, over six feet tall, with red eyes and a pair of enormous wings sprouting from its shoulders. Confronted with this horrifying sight, the women began to cry; it was quickly decided that a retreat back across the Kanawha River to West Virginia would be the best idea. Their journey was far from pleasant. Despite driving at speeds upwards of 100 mph, the car could not escape the strange creature, which made high-pitched squeals as it relentlessly pursued the vehicle down Route 62. The creature desisted only after the car entered the city limits of Point Pleasant.

After the police were summoned, they began a search of the marshy areas in which the sightings had taken place. They didn't find anything, but by morning the Scarberrys, the Mallettes and the alleged creature had become the punchline of a joke neither couple found at all amusing. Why, after all, would they concoct such a story? Why would they fabricate a hoax and invite the censure of the whole community of Point Pleasant? But if there was in fact no creature, how else could one explain the sudden disappearance of all the pigeons in the deserted plant where the creature was first seen? In spite of the skepticism, the couples soon learned that many people believed or at least wanted to believe in the phenomenon that became known as the Mothman.

That same evening, Newell Partridge, who lived 90 miles from Point Pleasant, experienced something quite unusual. He was watching his television when its images were replaced by a weird pattern. From outside, he heard a strange, screeching sound that slowly rose in pitch until silence fell over his farm once again. Partridge went out to investigate and saw that his guard dog's attention was firmly fixed on something by the hay barn. Partridge shone his flashlight over the general area and stopped when he saw two red orbs. It seemed that he had come face to face with the Mothman; mysteriously, its eyes didn't resemble an animal's. Partridge's dog, ever vigilant, ran off in pursuit of the creature. The dog was never seen again.

The next evening, a family in the area noticed a red light low in the sky, hovering above the TNT factory. They could offer no explanation. On her way for a visit, a friend of the same family noticed the same lights from her car. When she arrived at the home, she became terrified when she noticed a figure lying nearby. The creature rose from the ground, and the witness was struck by its glowing red eyes. The woman was beset by terrifying nightmares and visions for months, convinced that the Mothman was visiting her home.

Just days after the sighting was reported in area newspapers, the McClintic Wildlife Sanctuary experienced a jump in its number of visitors. More than 1000 people arrived to scour the marsh, some armed with flashlights and car headlights, others with shotguns and automatic rifles. They trekked across the many intersecting roads in search of the unknown, hoping to add themselves to growing list of people who claimed to have seen the Mothman. Besides the Mallettes and the Scarberrys, sightings had were reported in Cheshire, Rutland and Dodridge County in West Virginia. The Cheshire resident claimed that he had been chased down Route 7 in Ohio. Residents in the area surrounding the plant said that the creature watched them from behind a pile of bricks only to fly away moments later.

Those seeking a rational explanation for the Mothman turned to the scientific community. Dr. Robert Smith, a West

Virginia University biology professor, proposed that the Mothman was nothing more than a sandhill crane, a bird commonly found not in Ohio but in the Mexican Gulf region and in Canada. It probably got lost during a migratory flight and found its way to Ohio. Smith pointed out that the crane is six feet in height and can have a wingspan of 80 inches. As for the red glowing eyes, the crane's eyes weren't red, but its eyes were encircled by many red feathers. It would be easy to mistake the patches for eyes in the same way that people might do so with the white patches on killer whales. But those who believed in the Mothman wanted little to do with Smith's explanation. They had witnessed something unique, and they would not be denied the legitimacy of that experience. Other events began to command undue attention, however insignificant they might actually be. One woman, for instance, claimed that she'd seen a vision of the Mothman—that the creature would appear and frighten people, but not harm a soul.

In a January 1979 *Post* article, Frank Stanley reported that an eight-pound, gold-colored ball was found in Jackson County, West Virginia. It was hailed as solid evidence confirming the existence of the Mothman. The ball was an egg, undoubtedly the sort from which the Mothman must have sprung. The precious object was placed in a bank vault for security. But had an egg really been found? Despite expectations to the contrary, the egg was revealed as a hoax. A scoutmaster got wind of the egg, heard its description and came to the bank to examine the object. After it was proven to be a shot put, it was promptly returned to the scoutmaster.

With time, reported sightings of the Mothman dropped. Coincidentally enough, one of the last people to report

Point Pleasant Bridge, not far from where the mysterious Mothman of Mason County was first spotted

seeing the creature was Mabel McDaniel, Linda Scarberry's mother. But the debate over what the Mothman represented continued—a debate fueled by tragedy and speculation.

Twenty years before Point Pleasant was incorporated as a town, a great battle took place on its land. Fearful of colonial insurgents, Loyalist Virginia Governor Lord Dunmore sought to create a conflict between the colonials and Native Americans and thereby divert attention from the question of independence from the British Empire. With the promise of a peace treaty, he lured a multi-tribal confederation led by the Shawnee warrior Cornstalk to the point where the Kanawha and the Ohio Rivers converged. It was a ruse, and when the confederation of Native Americans arrived, they were ambushed by Virginia militiamen led by Andrew Lewis. Casualties were heavy on both sides, but when the day was over, the militiamen had handed the confederation a massive and crushing defeat. As Cornstalk lay dying on the field, he uttered a curse, condemning the area for 200 years. Cornstalk continues to haunt Point Pleasant and Kanauga, Ohio. He is remembered whenever tragedy strikes.

He was certainly invoked following the events of December 15, 1967, when the Silver Bridge collapsed just after 5 PM. The bridge was full of commuters traveling to and from Kanauga and Point Pleasant, West Virginia. Forty-six were sent to their deaths when an eyebar on the north side of the bridge failed, causing its suspension chain to drop and throwing the weight of the entire structure onto the southern chain. It could not hold. The eyebar that failed was numbered 13. To some, the bridge collapse was the climax of a cycle of eerie events that had been taking place in the months leading up to the disaster.

In addition to the Mothman sightings, people also reported that electrical appliances such as telephones and televisions were malfunctioning. Near the TNT plant, some cars would stall for no apparent reason. When inspected by mechanics, no reasonable explanation for their failure could be found. Strangers began arriving in Point Pleasant, their behavior arousing suspicion and fear in those who observed them. They inquired after the unexplained lights, claiming to be people that they obviously weren't. One man, dressed in a black suit with a black tie and claiming to be a reporter from Cambridge, Ohio, appeared at several homes, but accidentally let slip that he didn't know where Columbus was, despite it being just two miles from Cambridge. Allegedly, on the night that the Silver Bridge collapsed, a family living near the TNT plant noted more than 12 lights flashing overhead—lights that vanished as suddenly and inexplicably as they had appeared. Given Cornstalk's curse, the sightings of the Mothman might very well lend credence to the belief that something beyond our ability to comprehend took place. The story of the Mothman was immortalized in the film *The Mothman Prophecies*. But while the film claims that the Mothman was never sighted again in Point Pleasant and southeastern Ohio, some disagree.

Thirteen years after the initial sightings, in 1979, the Mothman was resurrected. Robert Ekey, writing in the *Athens Messenger*, reported on February 28, 1979, that Chet Buck of Athens and six other witnesses had seen a pair of large cranes along the Appalachian Highway. The cranes were six feet in height with wingspans of 10 feet and large red eyes. While Buck and others believed that they had encountered sandhill cranes, others claimed that the Mothman had returned. After all, they pointed out, sandhill cranes had never been seen in the area during the winter months. If they were to appear at all, it would be in April and October, not February. The fact that no regular bird watchers had seen the cranes also lent credence to the idea that Buck and the others had not seen a sandhill crane but had indeed caught a glimpse of the Mothman. This time, however, the excitement surrounding the sighting proved more subdued than in 1966. Once again, the story of the Mothman passed into legend, and one was left to wonder whether or not the Mothman ever really existed in the first place.

It's unlikely that anyone will ever know with full certainty what exactly the Scarberrys and the Mallettes saw on that fall evening in 1966. But for a short while, the people of south-eastern Ohio and West Virginia experienced something out of the ordinary—something that might even have been quite extraordinary.

The Wooster Steam Pumper

Wooster is a small community in Wayne County, the county seat of a rich agricultural area on the edge of Amish country. It is a college town where students come to study at a number of local postsecondary institutions. But Wooster is more. In some parts of the community, the past can come alive in ways one might not quite expect.

Wooster has always respected its firefighters. The city, after all, manufactures quite a large amount of firefighting equipment. The Wayne County Historical Society, at 546 East Bowman Street, even has a room that memorializes those who fight flames. On display is a hand pumper from 1831, a motorized steam engine from 1937 and a steam pumper from 1869. The steam pumper entered the society's collection on Memorial Day 2000. When in use, the machine was placed on a wagon and carted to a fire, where fire in its boiler would create steam to run its water pump. This represented a vast improvement over hand pumps. Wayne County Historical Society's steam pumper has quite a history, and how it came to be in Wooster is a tale of serendipity and good timing.

When the society began asking antiques collectors about a genuine steam pumper, they were guided by an old, time-worn photograph. The picture was one of the second steam pumper acquired by the Wooster Fire Department in 1869, purchased in part with city funds for the use of Relief Company 4. It had been manufactured in the east by Allerton, and considering that the company only produced the steam pumpers for a couple of years, it was a rare piece of equipment indeed. The machines were used right up until 1915, when they were replaced and rendered obsolete by

Historical photograph of the antique steam pumper that many Wooster residents consider haunted

motorized steam engines. Wooster lost track of Relief Company 4's steam pumper. It disappeared during the Second World War and all assumed that it had, in all likelihood, been sold for scrap—at least until early in 2000.

At that time, the society got a phone call from a collector in Pennsylvania, claiming to have an Allerton pumper. Naturally, those who went to see the pumper were quite excited, and even more so when they realized that what they were looking at was the pumper that had gone missing from the Wooster Fire Department so many years ago. There, on its blue glass lantern in white lettering, were the words: Relief Company 4. What once was lost had been found again. The trip had turned out better than anyone in the Wayne County Historical Society could have hoped for.

Having set out to find any old steam pumper, they uncovered one of their very own.

In the 1960s, a collector used to drive home from college in Indiana with his father, shopping for antiques along the way. One day, while driving along a rural back route, the pair stumbled upon the steam pumper in a barnyard. After they acquired it, they sent it east to Pennsylvania, where it was used to promote the family business. Finally, the pumper was returning home, despite some competition from the New York Fire Department.

Before the pumper assumed its place in the equipment room of the society, it was restored and repaired by the Wooster Fire Department. It was taken to Station Number 1 off North Market Street. At this point, the pumper's history begins a new chapter, but one distinctly wedded to its past.

One night, at around 1 AM, a firefighter was folding towels in the apparatus room when he was overcome by the sensation that he was being watched. He stopped folding and peered out of the corner of his eye. There, through a window and by the pumper, he saw a man. But he wasn't just any ordinary man. He was wearing a uniform in a style that hadn't been worn or seen in years. According to Doug Myers, a records officer with the fire department, the man was clad in an old-fashioned blue fire department uniform.

Hours later on the same evening, the leader on the late-night shift had a strange and unusual encounter as well. The building had been secured and silence fell over the station—the perfect accompaniment to a building now swathed in darkness. The shift leader got into bed and lay down, but then bolted upright suddenly. From his bed, he could hear what sounded like a group of men downstairs; their boisterous conversation and joyous laughter rose up to meet his ears.

Thinking the squad had returned, the officer padded down the stairs to greet his colleagues. But the minute the officer set foot into the apparatus room, the voices ceased. The squad hadn't returned and the officer soon realized he was the only person, at least living, in the building.

Myers, a self-proclaimed ghost hunter, was eager to record some evidence of the steam pumper and its ghosts. He set up a camera to take pictures of the pumper but when he got his rolls developed, he found that all he had were 40 pictures of the pumper. No orbs, no shadowy figures, nothing. "But," Myers says, "the nights were loud and busy. Maybe they were scared off."

Soon enough, more eerie events happened. The pumper was finally restored and brought to its new home at the Wayne County Historical Society. Members of the society began to experience some of what the firefighters had. The pumper, it seemed, had acquired something more than just rust and age during the intervening years. The theory is that members of Relief Company 4 have returned along with their equipment, happy that their machine is back in town. Figures have been sighted around the pumper, only to disappear when confronted. One time, a figure was mistaken for a historical society volunteer. When told that the only volunteer around at the time was in a different building, the witness' face "went dead white."

In July 2001, people heard something above their heads, a sound that floated above and out again. The sound has been described as a "low, throaty tone" that sounds very much like an old-fashioned alarm. A call was placed to Doug Myers. The people asked him if the pumper had a siren or alarm of any sort. Myers replied that it did, that the pumper had a steam whistle. The people were momentarily relieved to hear that their imaginations hadn't been playing tricks on them. But moments later, Myers told them that while the pumper had a whistle, the whistle was inoperable. Its mechanism was still housed at the station and the man in charge of the pumper's restoration had disconnected all tubes running to the steam whistle.

"We wanted to run the boiler, but the restoration was too expensive," says Myers. More importantly, no one had wanted to restore the boiler and risk operating the machine. Just months earlier, an antique steam tractor had exploded at a fair, killing six. All steam-powered vehicles and antiques were then dismantled. Without the boiler, there could be no fire, no water and therefore no pressure to blow the whistle.

People at the society were boggled; if the whistle wasn't operational, then what had they heard? The sound couldn't have been from one of the many diesel trucks that rattled and heaved their way through the back alley behind the complex; they emitted a far different sound. A quick examination of the equipment room revealed that there was no draft or breeze that could have blown over the whistle to create the sound. It was quickly decided that the men of Relief Company 4 were blowing the whistle. But that wasn't all they were up to.

In an experience similar to that of the late-night shift leader, someone at the society heard two men talking on the building's porch. The society wasn't open to visitors that day, but when someone walked into the hallway to relate that fact, the voices stopped and no men were there. The place, for all intents and purposes, was empty.

Ever since the pumper entered the historical society's collection, strange things have been happening. The doorbell rings even though no one is at the door. Alarms and motion detectors have been set off when the building is dark, quiet and empty.

The Wooster steam pumper is a rarity. The Allerton company made very few of them, and Myers believes that it is the only one from Allerton still in existence today. It is a link to the city's past in more ways than one. The spirits that seem to have found new life with the pumper's restoration will continue to serve the people of Wooster.

The Loveland Frog

Cryptozoology resembles zoology in every way, except that the objects of study—the animals—for the most part do not exist. Or rather, their existence has yet to be proven empirically. Given the limited scope of traditional zoology, perhaps it is not so unreasonable to argue that some creatures defy logic because of their radical uniqueness. A good analogy is explaining snow to a bushman from the Kalahari Desert. In the case of the Loveland Frog, it is best to suspend disbelief and listen to the story with an open mind.

In the 1950s, as a man was driving along a country road near Loveland, he suddenly slammed on his brakes, having seen something out of the side of his window. He pulled the car over and stared at what stood on the side of the road. He saw what he could only describe as frog creatures—three of them, all standing in a row. They resembled humans except that they had the heads of frogs and dark, leathery skin. Unsure what to do, the driver sat and then watched as one of the creatures produced something like a wand and used it to create glowing sparks. After three minutes, he'd had enough and left to report what he'd seen to the police department, but even after an extensive search by police chief John Fritz, none of the strange creatures he'd seen were ever found. Although people wondered what the man had seen, no answers were forthcoming. It wasn't until 1972, 20 years after the first sighting, that the frog creatures were seen once again roaming the sides of country roads.

Two sightings in March 1972 vaulted the Loveland Frog from a curiosity to a bona fide phenomenon. Cryptozoologists and others began to wonder if the frog humanoid really existed. What lent the two sightings such credibility was that they were reported by two police officers.

The first incident took place on March 3 when a police officer, who is sometimes named Ray Shockey, was driving along Riverside Road in the early hours of the morning. He stopped his car when he saw something he assumed to be a dog lying in the middle of the road. His headlights focused in on the still form. At that moment, the creature stood up to reveal itself. It was a large frog-like being, about three to four feet tall, between 50 to 75 pounds, human in shape but frog-like in form. It then jumped over the road's guardrail and disappeared down an embankment into the Miami River below.

The officer wasted no time returning to his station where he promptly grabbed another officer to return to the scene and carry out a thorough investigation. All they could find were tracks leading down the embankment into the river. With nothing concrete to report, the officer never filed a report on the incident.

Nor was a report filed two weeks later when another officer spotted a dead animal on Loveland Road. He decided to move it so that it wouldn't trouble other drivers. Yet when he approached the creature, it stood up and revealed itself as

A number of witnesses, including two police officers, spotted humanoid frog creatures on country roads near the Miami River.

some sort of man-frog. Some reports claim that the frog approached the officer menacingly, leading the officer to pull out his sidearm and fire four shots at it. Another account claims that the creature stood up at first but then crouched and made its way over to the side of the road, all the while keeping its eyes tightly trained on the officer. The policeman fired but missed, scaring the man-frog into fleeing over the guardrail and down into the Miami River.

Twenty-nine years later, the veracity of this sighting was called into question. Davy Russell, editor of the *X-Project*, interviewed the officer in question in 2001. Retired officer Mark Mathews claimed that "the entire thing has been…blown out of proportion. It was and is no monster…the animal I saw was…some type of lizard that either got too large for its aquarium or escaped by accident." Considering that no reports were ever filed concerning the incident and that Mathews was the only person on site to witness what took place, his explanation of events must be accepted. But his interpretation does not dismiss the mysteries and questions about the Loveland Frog.

In 1955, Darwin Johnson was swimming in the Ohio River when she felt something grab her leg and drag her under the surface. Whatever it was had claws; she could feel them digging sharply into her flesh. Johnson struggled to get away from her attacker but couldn't fight for long. Unlike her unseen assailant, she was distinctly out of her element. It wasn't until she was able to get her hands on a friend's inner tube that she broke free of the creature. When she examined her leg, it was marked with several cuts and a large green stain, shaped very much like a palm print.

There have been other sightings of the strange creature throughout the years, but none nearly as detailed or as vivid as those that took place in the 1950s and 1970s in Loveland. Although the mystery remains, drivers should be alert on that country road near the Miami River. A dead animal on the road might very well be the infamous Loveland Frog.

The Phantom Ship of Pymatuning

It is an area of Ohio rich in history, where the past lingers in a number of ways—in landscape, name and memory. And in one particular case, the past is still quite present, a spiritual echo still resounding after almost 170 years.

The area known as Pymatuning was shaped 14,000 years ago by great glaciers that covered the land. When the ice finally receded, it left a terrain pockmarked with dozens of kettle lakes. As time passed, a swamp forest developed as bogs, wetlands and stands of white pines became ever more prominent. Such a rich environment, abundant in resources, drew wild animals to the area; humans soon followed. It's said that the area was once inhabited by the Mound Builders, in a time of legend, and then by Native Americans. In time, European settlers began to make their way to the Pymatuning.

Initially, settlers from the east were intimidated by the land, the large swamp and an unforgiving and almost impenetrable forest. Only those whose greed bred the necessary motivation to survive came to Pymatuning—specifically, European fur traders who came in search of valuable beaver pelts. But as American cities in the east flourished, expansion into the harsh Pymatuning became a necessity. The area's stands of white pines attracted lumbermen eager to turn a profit. Shipbuilders prized the strong, straight trunks of the trees for their use in constructing sail masts. And, in keeping with a strong North American tradition, the European settlers honored the land's indigenous population by keeping the name given the area by the Native Americans, but drove the tribes away. Pymatuning, an Iroquois word, means "the crooked-mouthed man's dwelling place."

As competing groups jockeyed for land and claims, armed conflict between the two became a way of life on the frontier. And while the United States was now a nation, it was a fledging one at best, and the British Empire was still intent on bringing the revolutionaries back into their fold. British armies, recognizing the importance of tribes who knew the terrain and whose guerilla-style tactics had proven far superior to their own, curried the favor of Indian tribes to harass American settlers up and down the Ohio. It wasn't until the Iroquois and the Wyandot signed a treaty at Fort McIntosh, ceding land north of the Ohio River to Pennsylvania, that settlers from Connecticut and New York felt secure in moving into the area.

The rapid influx of white immigrants into northern Ohio stripped the Pymatuning area of much of its wilderness character, and it faded into the past. But late in the 19th century, a survey was conducted to determine the cost of reclaiming the Pymatuning swamp lands. The people of both Ohio and Pennsylvania were unwilling to part so quickly with their past, seeking to resurrect the long-dormant spirit of the swamp that had haunted them for so long.

Sometime in the late 18th or early 19th century, legend claims that a galley, measuring 60 feet long and 12 feet tall, sailed through the swamp. It was a foggy day with low visibility, and the galley struck something that it should have avoided and would have done so had conditions been different. The doomed galley and its crew disappeared in the swamps of Pymatuning, not to be seen again until another foggy night many years later. People around Pymatuning Lake began reporting that something could be seen out on the lake on foggy nights. Silhouetted by strange lights that appeared to come from nowhere, a ship cut through the fog and wended its way across the waters of the Pymatuning. With its timbers rotted away, the lost galley has apparently risen from the depths to sail once again.

Today, Pymatuning is the jewel of the park that bears its name—a natural playground with opportunities for camping, hunting and other recreational activities that, oddly enough, were essential for survival so many years ago. On foggy nights, however, a certain galley making its way through the mist serves as a ghostly reminder of those who didn't survive.

Serpent Mound

Societies need not only be haunted by ghosts; in many places, structures and monuments of ancient cultures and civilizations continue to haunt the inner chambers of the mind. These remnants of bygone marvels give rise to explanations sometimes too extraordinary to contemplate. The Egyptian pyramids. Stonehenge. The giant heads of Easter Island. Such awe-inspiring achievements question long-held assumptions regarding technology, progress and even extra-terrestrial beings. It is the same with a particular structure in southeastern Ohio.

Forty miles southwest of Chillicothe is long rounded pile of earth beneath a coverlet of spring-green grass. The mound is two to five feet high, nearly 20 feet wide and coils upon itself in seven folds for a quarter mile. Seen from the ground, it is hardly impressive, since the mound's undulations present only a subtle departure from the rolling hills of the surrounding landscape. But seen from the air, and in particular from the site's viewing tower, the form becomes a gigantic serpent, constructed from earth, with its mouth wrapped around a disc, its body folded seven times, its tail a tight coil. Lying on a plateau overlooking the valley of Brush Creek, the Serpent Mound is the largest effigy of its kind in the United States. Years after its rediscovery, the mound continues to present mysteries that confound the curious.

It is not clear how old the mound really is. The absence of any relics or artifacts within the serpent has prevented any attempts by archaeologists to prove definitively when the mound was built. Before radiocarbon tests were conducted, speculation relied upon the fact that conical burial mounds of the Adena people had been found in the area, the legacy of

Of uncertain age and origins, Serpent Mound in southeastern Ohio has baffled scientists for generations.

a civilization that inhabited an area stretching from what is now the Midwest to the Atlantic coast. Implements and artifacts found in their burial mounds reveal that the prehistoric Adena flourished between 800 BC and 100 AD. But in 1996, samples were taken from the mound's core, where radiocarbon dating was performed on bits of wood charcoal. These findings moved the mound's construction date forward by almost 2000 years, to about 1100 AD. Theorists attributed the Serpent Mound to the Fort Ancient people, a Mississippian group that lived in the central Ohio Valley from 900 to 1600. They moved freely among the Tennessee,

Cumberland and Mississippi Valleys, growing maize and constructing grand earthen works. To lend further support to this hypothesis was the discovery of the remains of a Fort Ancient village just 100 yards south of the mound. Of course, there are those who disagree with this proposed solution to the mystery.

Ross Hamilton believes that to rely on carbon-dating would be folly. No wood, burned or not, was used in the construction of the mound; therefore, any charcoal found within would be the result of "formation processes"—burrowing animals carrying materials from the ground to the land below. Hamilton dates the creation of the Serpent Mound to the time when Egyptian pharaohs were erecting their massive pyramids in Giza, a time when the polestar was not Polaris, but Thuban. This fact is central to Hamilton's theory that the Serpent Mound is Thuban-centric, with Polaris rising to become the polestar only after years of slow wobbling in the earth's axis, displacing earth's views of the constellations above ever slowly.

Regardless of the Serpent Mound's age, it is closely linked with all the celestial bodies of the sky: the stars, the sun and the moon. Those who believe it was built sometime in the 11th century focus on two extraordinary events that might serve as explanations for the drive to construct the mounds. In 1054, light from the supernova that created the Crab Nebula reached earth—a brilliant illumination of the night and day sky that remained for two weeks. Then, in 1066, while William the Conqueror was raiding the shores of England, Halley's Comet made its brightest appearance ever. Others speculate that several eclipses would have been seen by the builders of the mound—phenomena represented by the image of the serpent swallowing the sun. In fact, features of the Serpent Mound are closely aligned with both the summer solstice sunset and the winter solstice sunrise, the first known coupling of both solar and lunar events in an effigy. The Serpent Mound provides evidence of an attempt to unite night and day, light and dark, good and evil. It is a monument to heaven, earth and the underworld.

Its importance to its creators cannot be understated. In January 1999, Philip and Phylis Morrison wrote in *Scientific American* that it would have taken years to construct the great serpent. A few hundred able-bodied workers would have carried close to 300,000 loads of local soil on their backs to the mound site to be shaped and formed. With only a few pleasant weeks each year in which to work after harvest, the workers would have spent five to ten seasons constructing the mound, an effort requiring great patience, care and dedication.

William F. Romain, an archaeologist, points out in great detail how greatly the serpent looms within the folklore of numerous North American Indian cultures. Many varied legends explain an eclipse as the result of a serpent attacking the sun and swallowing it. The serpent is a malevolent creature that rises from the depths of hell to challenge the light above. A variety of topographical features surrounding the Serpent Mound tie in closely with mythological beliefs concerning heaven and hell. The caves, sinkholes and springs of the area were believed to be entrances to the underworld, as Brush Creek may have been. The creek lies just west of the mound. Rivers, lakes and streams were often connected with the underworld, a symbol of the unknown. Seen in this light, the Serpent Mound is an expression of the duality of life, of a world where human beings inhabit a realm neither good nor evil, but one pitched between heaven and hell.

While the Serpent Mound is not haunted in the conventional sense, it is a distinct link with a distant past—the very articulation of questions that haunt us now as much as they did those who have long since stopped walking the earth. In the Serpent Mound, one finds not only a connection to the past, but also a kinship with the anxieties and concerns that encompass all cultures. What haunts the soul is a recognition of the familiar within the exotic.

The Mummy Cat

Cats have long held a special place in the heart. The ancient Egyptians worshipped the creatures as a deities, and people today continue to turn to the animals for companionship, solace and comfort. For a lighthouse keeper's wife, cats were her only company as she drifted in out and of consciousness in her futile fight against an illness that would eventually claim her life. While most of her cats were given away or sold after she died, at least one chose to remain behind and continues to roam the living quarters where it must have provided much needed comfort in the wife's final days.

At the Fairport Harbor Historical Society's museum, the past comes to life in its collection of antiques. Created in 1945, the lighthouse museum on the east side of the Grand River was the first of its kind along the Great Lakes and in the United States. It was a fitting way to memorialize two structures, built in 1825 and then again in 1871, that had been scheduled for demolition in 1941.

In 1925, the head of the Bureau of Lighthouses, George Putnam, saw no reason to keep the lighthouse. He earmarked ten thousand dollars for its demolition, and only the impassioned pleas of locals saved the building. In 1941, just when things looked their bleakest, Fairport again saved its lighthouse when the citizenry proposed that the building serve the community good. Fairport was granted a probationary leave of five years, and the museum opened for business in 1946. So while the lighthouse no longer guides sailors to safe harbor, the building now lights the way to the past—to a kinship with previous generations now lost.

Settlers from the east first began arriving on the Lake Erie shore when the Connecticut Land Company opened up 120

Long associated with the Babcock family, this lighthouse overlooking Lake Erie is now part of the Fairport Harbor Museum.

miles of land along the shorefront. The area became known as the Western Reserve, and homesteaders and speculators came to reap the benefits of arable land and bountiful game. They named their flourishing settlement Grandon, in honor of the Grand River, a name adopted from the French explorers who first had their settlements here and christened the waterway "La Grande Riviere." Traffic on both the river and Lake Erie increased so steadily that a lighthouse had become a necessity by 1825. Since no decent roads existed as settlers made their way from western New York and Pennsylvania, most were forced to travel by river. The little settlement had become important as both a fueling station and a supply harbor for ships headed out to other ports. Grandon also decided that it was time for a new name, something that might draw even more people to the region. Fairport seemed appropriate.

The lighthouse would be placed at the mouth of the Grand River, overlooking Lake Erie. Notices were placed in local newspapers asking for bids on the proposed development. Specifications included a stone or brick tower 30 feet tall and a two-story house with a cellar and well. Jonathon Goldsmith, a Connecticut native, won the contract to build the lighthouse and keeper's quarters for $2900. In the fall of 1825, he had completed construction of both, but asked for more money when he realized that a cellar was part of the deal. The city was far from enthusiastic in meeting Goldsmith's demands, but there was little they could do; they wanted their cellar and hiring another contractor was out of the question. In the end, Goldsmith ended up pocketing almost double his original fee. He walked away from the job with over five thousand dollars, but he had burned his bridges.

A decade later, the foundation of the tower had settled so dramatically that replacing it, at great cost and time, had become a necessity. Six years later, when the search for a lighthouse keeper was conducted, Goldsmith applied for the job in one of those sublime moments of poetic justice. Not surprisingly, his application was rejected. The job went instead to Samuel Butler, an ardent abolitionist who would be the first of 17 keepers to serve at the lighthouse.

Under Butler's watch, the lighthouse became more than just a beacon of safety. As one of the main points on the northern terminals of the Underground Railway, it became a symbol of hope. Just as the Statue of Liberty stood for a promise of freedom for the millions of immigrants who passed through Ellis Island, so too did the light at Fairport Lighthouse indicate that fugitive slaves were approaching a new life in Canada. Slaves passed through the harbor on

The mummified cat that haunts the museum once belonged to Mrs. Babcock.

boats loaded down with goods such as oil of peppermint and upright pianos.

By 1868, the lighthouse had fallen into a state of great disrepair; one of the iron bands supporting the weight of the tower had snapped and braces were needed to ensure that the structure survived the harsh Ohio winter. A new lighthouse was needed. On April 4, 1870, work began on the new structure, but it was halted when funds were frozen. The building was left untouched for almost a year. When work resumed in 1871, the structure had already begun to deteriorate. An extra $10,000 was needed to complete the project.

When completed, the new tower stood 70 feet tall, had a spiral iron staircase of 69 steps and began a long association with the Babcock family. Captain Joseph Babcock was the first keeper of the new lighthouse, and despite escaping death time and time again, it seemed that death might claim one of those close to him instead. At eight years old, Babcock escaped being killed during an Indian attack in Sandusky because his mother was Indian. Later, he served in the Civil War. He survived the conflict, only to see one of his children, Robbie, die at the age of five of smallpox. Then his wife fell ill and spent a long period of time bedridden in the second floor quarters of the lighthouse. Her days were brightened by the presence of numerous cats. After the captain passed on, his position was filled by son Daniel, who stayed as head keeper until 1925, when the lighthouse was decommissioned. Even now, years later, the museum retains the unmistakable legacy of the Babcocks.

It's been said that son Robbie continues to haunt the museum. Staff claim that cold air and the smell of decay are very strong in the basement, as is a sense of dread. Perhaps more interesting is Mrs. Babcock's cat, which is truly something special.

The cat, of course, has been dead for years. What the volunteers, employees and historians of the lighthouse see in the old living quarters is actually a spirit—the ethereal remains of what was once a gray puff cat. During a renovation in the winter of 2001, its body was found in a basement crawl space. A worker was climbing through an open area in the basement when he felt something brush his head. When he looked at what it was, he was startled to see the preserved remains of a gray cat. The workers had no idea what to do with their discovery and left the animal at the foot of the stairs.

"I didn't know a cat had been found," says Carol Bertone, a publicist for the museum. "I went downstairs and there it was, propped at the bottom of the stairs, staring at me. I screamed and ran up the stairs. It had paws, eyelashes, whiskers, leathery skin. All the features were still there. Everything was still intact." It was obvious that the cat had been laying on its side when it died. No one knows how old the cat is, but it was perfectly preserved by the conditions in the dark, cold lighthouse basement. When word about the discovery spread, it lent credence to the rumors that a cat haunted the lighthouse. The story had been circulating for a while, but skeptics refused to believe in the ghost until the discovery of the mummified cat that so closely matched earlier reports.

Former curator Pamela Brent fervently affirms its existence. She told the *Plain Dealer* in May 2001 that "it would skitter across the floor near the kitchen, like it was playing. I would catch glimpses of it from time to time." Brent lived in the lighthouse for four years and claimed that one evening, while lying in bed, she felt something jump on her bed. She looked around but didn't see anything, and was certain that the cat was present when she could feel its weight pressing down on her. After her initial encounters with the gray cat, Brent was a little "freaked out." Now, she has accepted the spirit world as just another plane of existence. Bertone has never experienced anything quite like Brent, and she has yet to see the museum's phantom feline, but she still says that at night "it feels eerie in the room."

For now, Bertone will have to wait. And while the mummified cat aroused the interest of people from Pennsylvania to San Francisco and drew crowds of visitors, some volunteers at the museum feel the cat should be moved to another location. Some were worried about bacteria while others feared reactions from those with weak constitutions. Bertone protested, fighting to keep what she considered "our pet" in the museum. After all, tours and school-age children all wanted to come and see the ghost cat. Unfortunately, while Bertone was away one day, someone picked up the preserved pet and whisked it away from the only home it had ever known.

Bertone hopes that the mummified cat will eventually find its way back to the Fairport Harbor Museum. Until that day, employees and visitors of the lighthouse will have to content themselves with the cat's spirit, still alive and well after all these years.

2
Haunted Houses and Hotels

~

We like to think of our bedrooms as secure, private places—havens where we can escape the pressures of our daily lives. These places are meant to be our Edens, our own little utopias. In the daily comings and goings of our lives, we rarely consider that we might very well be snakes in someone else's garden, that we might be disturbing the peace of others. Houses and hotels develop a character all their own over time, retaining various elements from their own particular pasts. For the most part, these elements are apparent in decor and architectural design. But every now and then, a building's past will reveal itself in unexpected ways. Previous inhabitants, who prefer not to go quietly into that good night, choose to remain long after death. It's a living arrangement that makes for some spirited stories.

~

Punderson Manor

A stay in a room at Punderson Manor can be an unusual experience. The room, for starters, is gorgeous—for once it looks just like the picture in the brochure. The hotel seems like the perfect place from which to explore the bucolic splendor of northeastern Ohio. Of course, to enjoy the wilderness and the hotel's amenities, you must able to leave the room. For one unfortunate couple staying at Punderson Manor, they couldn't even do that.

Upon checking into the Windsor Suite, a man and a woman were overjoyed by its elegance. The husband wandered around the living area while the wife went into the bedroom to lie down. Only when she tried to get up again, she couldn't. Later, she said she felt as if several people were sitting on her, that the weight bearing down upon her made it impossible to move. She was able to escape when her husband came into the room and saw the look of absolute terror on her face. Taking his wife by the hand, he pulled her off the bed easily. The couple returned to the front desk, eager to leave. The husband was perplexed by the behavior; his wife was a stable person. But for the veteran staff at the Punderson, it was no mystery. One of its many resident ghosts had struck again.

The Punderson Manor Resort and Conference Center boasts an 18-hole championship golf course, a swimming pool, tennis and basketball courts, as well as facilities for boating, fishing, hiking and jogging, all set within the woods of Geauga County. Less than an hour away from Cleveland, Punderson can provide a welcome escape from the pressures of living in an urban metropolis. So comfortable is the place that some have decided never to leave, refusing to allow death to prevent them from walking the hallways of the old Tudor mansion.

Karl Long, a millionaire from Detroit, came to Geauga County in 1929. He began construction on a 29-room, 14-bath mansion that would eventually become Punderson Resort. Theories differ as to why Long sought escape in Geauga, but two of the more popular ones propose that either his wife was not fond of Detroit or that Long needed desperately to get away from his work in a pre-Depression business. Regardless of his motivation, the home was never completed. Like countless other Americans, Long lost his fortune when the Great Depression ravaged the American economy. Without the necessary funds, he had to abandon his dreams. Some say he was so devastated by his loss that he hanged himself in the uncompleted home's attic. In the end, the property he had purchased reverted back to Dr. Coopedge, the original owner and a descendant of the W.B. Cleveland family, before ending up in the hands of the state.

Construction on the mansion was completed in 1956. Looking to profit from the investment, the state opened the residence up for lodging and dining, naming the complex Punderson in honor of Lemuel Punderson who, along with his wife Sybal, first settled the area in 1802. It wasn't long before the state was forced to expand the property, adding a wing with extra guest rooms and building 26 two-bedroom cabins. By the 1970s, Clevelanders were flocking to the resort, jumping at the chance to flee from the concrete jungle into the untamed wilderness just a short drive away. During this time, when Punderson Resort was just beginning to hit its stride, people began to believe that the place was haunted.

Over the years, a number of incidents have taken place in Punderson that cannot be explained rationally. Although the

1982 discovery of previously concealed rooms and passage-ways suggested that some of the reported incidents may have been staged, many others continue to defy all attempts at explanation.

A security officer and his partner had just checked the boiler in the basement to make sure that it was working properly. Satisfied, they began slowly working their way through the manor. Since the manor had just changed management, it was, for all intents and purposes, empty. As the two made their way up the circular staircase connecting the main lobby to the second floor, they heard what Linda Feagler of *Cleveland Magazine* called "a woman's shrieking laughter." Immediately after, the hallway became inexplicably cold—cold enough that the officers could see their breaths condensing in the 70-degree air. As soon as the laughter moved past the two of them, everything returned to normal. To this day, the pair cannot explain what happened that night.

In another incident, a restaurant hostess was napping on a couch when she was awakened by the sound of children laughing and jumping on the sofa. When she awoke and looked around, the room was empty. The children were nowhere to be found. Often, guests will be awakened from sleep by loud noises coming from rooms next to theirs. The catch, of course, is that when guests call down to the front desk to complain, they're sometimes told that those rooms are empty. One guest complained about a party taking place above his room; he must have forgotten that he was staying on the top floor.

In *Haunted Ohio II*, Chris Woodyard writes that the hotel staff even threw a party for the ghosts on Halloween in 1979. The staff dedicated a cake to "To the Ghosts of Punderson." It was a wild night, and the spirits fully embraced the opportunity to celebrate. Pictures fell form the wall, pens flew across the room and the activity continued well into the early hours of the morning, stopping only when the front door mysteriously opened and closed on its own. Although it was probably the sound of the spirits making their exits, by no means had they left for good.

Woodyard also writes about how one man was working one night when he noticed the papers on his desk blow away. He turned behind him to see a large floor fan hovering several feet above the floor, its blades whirring away. The fan continued its progress across the floor, but stopped when it unplugged itself. The fan gently settled itself on the floor. Connie Schultz reported in the December 19, 2000, edition of the *Plain Dealer* that the chandelier in the center hallway of the manor is often seen spinning by employees arriving to work early in the morning. A bartender, Mimi Napp, couldn't shake the feeling that something or someone was watching her whenever she counted the money in the cash drawer.

Not all encounters were so innocent. The strangest and most disturbing of all the stories took place in 1979, when three employees witnessed a gruesome apparition. They were talking into the early hours of the morning one night near the front desk. One of the three went to get a cup of coffee in the room that now serves as the manor's lounge. She returned shortly after, asking the other two, in awed and hushed tones, to come with her. The others soon saw what it was that had aroused such a strange reaction in their friend. There, before them, was the specter of a man dressed like a lumberjack, hanging by his neck from a rope that extended up towards the ceiling but disappeared before reaching it. The man rotated slowly on the rope, swaying gently to and fro.

The group watched the spectacle for nearly three hours, the image disappearing only in the light of a new day.

Who was the lumberjack? Some believe it's Karl Long, who allegedly hung himself so many years ago when the Depression robbed him of his wealth. And if it is Karl Long, then who are the other spirits? A number of guests keep hearing the voices of children. Who are they? Records show that no children ever lived in the home, and despite rumors about Long's suicide, there is no proof that anyone ever died in the home. As for the children, a longtime resident of Geauga County born in 1899 recounted that as a child, he heard about a tavern that burned down across the lake from the Punderson Manor in 1885. Allegedly, a number of the victims had been children. Perhaps they migrated across the lake to the comfort of the Punderson.

A psychic who examined the house claimed to have had a conversation with a spirit who looked a little Theodore Roosevelt and promised to haunt the home until his rocking chair was returned. The same longtime resident who remembered the burning of the tavern claimed that W.B. Cleveland, father-in-law of the man who sold Karl Long his land, looked a little like the former president, at least when it came to their mustaches. Eerily enough, the Geauga County Historical Society Museum has in its possession a rocking chair. It once belonged to Sybal Punderson, who brought it to Ohio by wagon from Connecticut. The chair was inherited by W.B. Cleveland, who is apparently still searching for the chair that was never returned.

It may never become completely clear who or what still haunts the Punderson Resort, but one would be hard-pressed to deny that there isn't something unusual happening there.

The Thurber House

People first saw it at nine in the evening. Twisted ribbons of black smoke wended and twirled into skies illuminated by moonlight. Then the people smelled it—the unmistakable scent of burning wood mixed with the musty aromas of a late fall evening. Plaintive wails of the helpless followed, causing dread and concern. Soon after, fire claxons joined the discordant symphony of crackling wood, shattering glass and pleading voices. Firefighters raced to the scene, as did Dr. S.M. Smith, the president of the board of trustees of the Central Ohio Lunatic Asylum. His building was on fire and full of individuals unable to help themselves or understand their peril.

Smith arrived to see firefighters swarming the asylum, desperately fighting their way to the amusement room where many of the inmates were. Breaking into the building, firefighters rescued as many of the patients as they could; some were taken from their sleep while others relished the opportunity to be free of their sick beds. Circumstances, however, wouldn't allow it. They were taken to the Deaf and Dumb Asylum in whatever was available, be it carriage, wagon or stagecoach. Seven were lost in an otherwise heroic rescue.

The firefighters stayed behind to battle the blaze but found that their best efforts would not save the building. Their greatest weapon, water, was in short supply. Some were dispatched to other areas to draw water from cisterns to replenish those at the site. The fire, weakened for a moment, roared back to life, consuming the asylum. A journalist who witnessed the event wrote the following on November 18, 1868: "The disaster is one of the most terrible kind. The announcement will strike the people at large, as it did the citizens of Columbus last night, with a terror that cannot be named." The incident has marked the area; it is still a place where the supernatural and the natural converge, as the following story of famous writer James Thurber shows.

After the blaze, the area was divided into three residential blocks, each centered on an elliptical park. Houses were constructed on the edge of what was then a fashionable area of Columbus known as East Park Place. A two-story house at 77 Jefferson Avenue was built in 1873 as a private residence; by the turn of the century, it had become a rental property, with tenants coming and going through its halls until 1973. In the 1920s, it served as the site of the Wallace Collegiate School and Conservatory of Music. Later, it became a boarding house. But of all the families and people to have lived in the home, the most loved and best known were the Thurbers.

Charles and Mary Agnes Thurber and their three sons, Robert, William and James, lived in the house from 1913 to 1917. Although the family moved quite often, the house on Jefferson is their most memorable. One evening, on the 44th or 47th anniversary of the terrible asylum disaster, James had an unusual experience. His story was recorded in *The Thurber House Organ* in August 1988. James' father and little brother were both out of town in Indianapolis, while his older brother was asleep. In all his life, James had never once entertained the notion that ghosts might exist; as an aspiring journalist, he dealt with fact, not fiction. But beliefs can change in an instant.

While drying his face, James heard something from down the stairs—the sounds of a man pacing around their dining room table. But no one was in the house besides James and his older brother; one was in the bathroom, the other was fast asleep. James' first thought was for his safety, and he feared that their home was being invaded by either a burglar or a crazy individual. Misery loves company and, apparently, so too does terror.

James woke up his older brother and took him to the home's back staircase, the one that led directly to the dining room and whomever might be pacing around the dining room table. As is often the case, though, the sounds stopped the minute James and his brother reached the landing. His older brother, annoyed at losing sleep over something so inconsequential, turned on James, asking what was wrong with him. Convinced he was not mistaken, James told his brother as much. Just as he finished speaking, heavy footfalls of a man approached from the stairs. But there was no man, only the sounds of someone leaping two steps at a time. The speed with which James' brother retreated into his bedroom was matched only by how quickly his skepticism faded. James, on the other hand, stood rooted at the top of the stairs until the last possible moment. Finally, when he could take it no more, he slammed the door at the top of the stairs shut. Suddenly, the non-existence of ghosts was very much in doubt. The house at 77 Jefferson Avenue certainly appeared to be haunted. But by whom?

James, a student at Ohio State University who also wrote for its paper, *The Lantern,* decided to investigate what happened in the house. The next day, he asked a local druggist if anything strange had ever happened in the house at 77 Jefferson.

The druggist looked at James, slightly incredulous, and said, "Didn't you know about the steps that go around the dining room table and run up the stairs?" Emboldened, James dug deeper into the home's past and discovered that a number of families had left the home because of the

On a staircase in his childhood home, a young James Thurber encountered the ghost of a man with a tragic past.

unexplained footsteps. Eventually, James uncovered the truth behind the haunting.

Years ago, a couple lived in the house. One day, while at work, the husband received a disturbing phone call from a strange voice. The unidentified person said that if the husband went home at ten that morning, he would find his wife in bed with another man. The husband returned home and stood in the dining room, listening for anything untoward. He heard her almost immediately. Unable to face his wife's infidelity, the husband paced around the dining room table and then raced up the staircase, entered one of the bedrooms and shot himself dead in the head. Even now, years later, the man is still reliving the worst morning of his life, pacing around the table only to rush up the steps to kill himself, again and again.

James was so moved by the experience that he later turned it into a story. By the late 1920s, he had become an editor of *The New Yorker* and was gaining acclaim for both his drawings and humorous writings. With the support and friendship of E.B. White, James was able to "learn discipline in writing…and realize [that] a writer turns on his mind, not a faucet." In 1933, he wrote a story for publication in the magazine called "The Night the Ghost Got In." The following is an excerpt:

> The ghost that got into our house on the night of November 17, 1915, raised such a hullabaloo of mis-understandings that I didn't just let it keep on walking and go to bed. Its advent caused my mother to throw a shoe through a window of the house next door and ended up with my grandfather shooting a patrolman. I am sorry, therefore, as I have said, that I ever paid any attention to the footsteps.

While he never referred directly to his old family home, to avoid frightening anyone who might be living there, his account popularized 77 Jefferson Avenue. While James lived there for only four years, the home has become forever linked with him. Thurber was a prolific writer and artist who compensated for his eventual blindness with an uncanny ability to hold as many as 2000 words in his head. He could compose, revise and edit prose without pen or paper. Thurber had a long and illustrious career at *The New Yorker,* and his best-known work is still *The Secret Life of Walter Mitty.*

77 Jefferson Street is now known as the Thurber House. It functions as a gallery and writers' center, and holds a place on the National Register of Historic Places. In 1976, the home was donated to the Jefferson Center for Learning and the Arts, an organization that began the restoration of the house. Exterior renovations began in November 1983 with funding from all over the United States and across the world; by March 1984, interior restoration began, a process aided greatly by the memories of Robert Thurber. It has sponsored readings and seminars by writers such as John Updike and Maxine Hong Kingston. For some, though, it is first and foremost a home. The ghosts within seem to remind visitors and staff alike that it wasn't only James who lived in the house.

Over the years, a number of people in the Thurber House have witnessed the strange and unusual. In 1987, according to accounts published in *The Thurber House Organ,* a man named O'Bear Thompson was playing Trivial Pursuit one evening. His wife read a question about the Thurber House, and although Thompson had never heard of the home before, something about the question struck something inside his memory. He swore that he had once lived in it when it was being used a boarding house in the 1960s. He lived alone in the attic, and the stairs from the second floor led to his room. But night after night, he'd lie in bed and hear footsteps walking up the steps and then down the steps. Although the footsteps would occasionally stop just outside his door, no one ever knocked. Because he never felt uneasy or afraid, Thompson never got out of bed to see if anyone might be there.

In 1992, an administrative assistant noticed the sound of a chair rolling overhead and then footsteps. The noises,

While on staff at The New Yorker, *Thurber published his account of the haunting under the title "The Night the Ghost Got In."*

innocuous enough on their own, attracted her attention because no one was upstairs at that particular time. When she walked by the bookstore shelves through the door between the living room and the bookstore, books mysteriously fell from the shelves behind her.

On another occasion, a maintenance contractor closed a closet door on the third floor and left the room. When he returned, the door was open. Questioning whether or not he had closed the door, the contractor simply closed the door again and went back to work. Later, he found the closet door open again. There was no doubt that he had closed it earlier. He closed the door and then tried to open it. But he couldn't. Even though the closet door had no lock, he couldn't pull the door open. He pulled again and again, and finally walked out of the house saying that he would not return "until the ghost quiets down."

A short time later, Thurber House's writer-in-residence moved into the third floor apartment. It wasn't long before she was alerting staff about the fussy closet. She also noticed that her radio would never stay off, turning itself back on mysteriously. Moreover, it was always tuned to a different station. Paula DiPerna, a writer-in-residence in 1988, wrote in *The Thurber House Organ* that she saw a ghost—a heavy-set being with stooped shoulders, dressed in a raincoat with the collar turned up. Later, she "heard unaccountable clattering of the lower kitchen cupboards."

It's difficult to say who the ghosts might be. The cuckolded husband, of course, comes to mind, but regarding those who pull books from shelves or turn radios on and open closet doors, identities remain a mystery. They might very well be the spirits of those who perished in the asylum fire of 1868, but that's only speculation. Whoever they are, perhaps they will one day inspire another writer like young James Thurber on the night the ghost got in.

Franklin Castle

Hannes Tiedemann was born in Germany in 1833. It's not known when he came to America, but he settled in the Near West Side of Cleveland, which was populated by German immigrants. He quickly found work as a barrel maker and soon met and fell in love with a woman named Luise. After the two young lovers were married, Hannes quit his barrel-making job and instead joined the Weideman Company, a wholesale grocery and liquor business. He needed to support what he anticipated would be a large family. By 1865, the Tiedemanns had enough money to begin construction on a new home. They chose a vacant lot at 4308 Franklin Boulevard on which to build their dreams.

When the house was finished, the Tiedemanns moved in. Their brood had multiplied during the wait, and Hannes and Luise were joined by his mother Wiebeka, his cousin Ludwick and a son, August. Just a year later, Emma became the latest addition to the Tiedemann clan. Hannes was 34 and Luise was 29. Many years passed happily inside the home that had been christened Franklin Castle.

At the age of 15, Emma finally lost a battle with diabetes. At least that was the official story. Just three months later, Hannes' mother, Wiebeka, already 84, also passed away. While no one ever questioned the causes of Wiebeka's death, some people speculated whether or not Hannes had a hand in Emma's death. Was it really diabetes that did his daughter in? Or was there something far more sinister at work? Although there are no facts to support the idea that Hannes hanged his daughter from the rafters of the fourth floor ball-room, the story has survived to become a part of Franklin Castle's mythology. Hannes, after all, had a reputation as a dominating, overbearing man who could be cruel and unpredictable. Legend also claims that a horrific murder involving an axe and a young woman took place in the front tower room. The woman, apparently, was a young servant girl who had been carrying on an affair with Hannes; she had been chopped to death by him in a fit of rage when he learned of her intentions to marry another. It's believed that when passers by look up at the front tower window, even now, they occasionally catch a glimpse of some shadowy figure— the ghost of the slain servant girl.

Murders and curiosity aside, two years later, in 1883, Luise decided that her home needed to be rebuilt. She contacted the architectural firm of Cudell and Richardson, who had just completed work on the Franklin Circle Church. Their work on the Tiedemann's house made it singularly unique. It was the only private residence the pair ever designed, and the home, rebuilt in the Romanesque Revival style, was one of the first of its kind in Cleveland and one of the very few left standing today. The home was finished with over 30 rooms and four floors, and decorated with numerous balconies and gables. They paid great attention to detail, making sure that each window had interior shutters fastened with hand-made hinges. Images of butterflies and birds were carved into each of them.

In 1895, Luise Tiedemann, who was reportedly a heavy drinker, died at 57 of liver trouble. Some suspected Hannes of having a role in her passing, claiming that he might have poisoned her. Her funeral was held in the front parlor of the castle, and her coffin was taken, by carriage, to Riverside Cemetery. Hannes, perhaps unwilling to live in a home where so much tragedy had taken place, sold Franklin Castle to a brewer from Buffalo. Tiedemann returned to Germany where he married a waitress named Henriette. He then returned again to America where he built a home on Lake Road. His marriage to Henriette was far from happy, and shortly before his death in 1908 from a stroke, he prevented his wife from ever inheriting any of his amassed wealth.

Franklin Castle was sold in 1913 to a German socialist party that used the home for parties and meetings; under their care, the home fell into disrepair. They gutted the interior, removing many of the home's original fixtures. A main staircase was removed and a bank entrance was bricked over. When a German short-wave radio was found in the rafters of the fourth floor, the discovery gave rise to stories of Nazi spies and of 20 people being gunned down in a hidden room. Franklin Castle, however, was largely unoccupied for the next 55 years. There was little during this period to suggest that the castle was haunted.

It wasn't until James Romano, his wife and six children took possession of the home in 1961 that strange things started happening. On the first day that they family moved in, Mrs. Romano was told by her children that they were not alone in the house. While playing on the fourth floor, the Romano children claimed to have encountered an oddly dressed little girl who spoke funnily. The child also refused to come downstairs, never venturing far from the fourth floor. But the children were not the only ones to receive a new friend; Mrs. Romano allegedly became quite close with the spirit of Luise Tiedemann. Some say the connection was only natural, since both were mothers of six children, with twins no less, and they both slept in the same room. Mrs. Romano believed that Luise had chosen her to be a confidant— someone in whom the spirit could place her deepest secrets. The two got along well and Mrs. Romano concluded that any spirits who might be haunting the home were protective and meant the family no harm. She was quite surprised to learn later that she might have been be mistaken.

When the Northeast Ohio Psychical Research Society visited the home, apparently one member was so disturbed by the presences within that he or she immediately fled the residence, never to return. The society determined that whatever it was that was haunting Franklin Castle was decidedly unfriendly. A Catholic priest was brought into the home and he too sensed an evil presence. When Mrs. Romano protested that she could not believe that Luise meant her family any harm, the priest countered that the spirits were only being kind so that they could gain her confidence and lure her into their clutches. For what purpose? No one knows. Shortly after, the family was warned of an impending death by the spirits. The Romanos moved out of the home, but the death still occurred.

In 1974, the home was purchased by Sam Muscatello. Muscatello opened the house to public tours, and while some claim that he actively courted the public and the media, inviting both to come to share and record their experiences, he is quoted in the May 11, 1975, edition of the *Cleveland Plain Dealer* as claiming that he only wanted to turn the home into a church. That is not to say that strange things didn't happen in the home.

A WEWS TV-5 News cameraman, Ted Ocepee, recalled in an article in the *Plain Dealer* that the ceiling lamp in one particular room in the house kept spinning around in a circle inexplicably. There was no draft in the room, and while traffic from the street might have caused the lamp to swing around, the house and the room both felt quite still. Ocepee wrote, "You can't be in the castle very long without feeling your heart start to pound for no reason." Human bones were found within the walls, but whether they were the remains of a hapless victim or had simply been planted by someone seeking to drum up publicity is still in question. Lights would blink on and off for no reason, doors would open and close of their own accord and soft voices were sometimes heard in otherwise empty rooms and halls. Muscatello took photos of specific rooms in the castle and noticed that some revealed the presence of orbs and unexplained shapes and lines.

Muscatello failed in his attempt to create his Universal Christian Church. His tour business suffered after a clandestine raid on the home during a fundraiser by police and state liquor agents. They charged four people with liquor violations, four others with resisting arrest and one with disorderly conduct. The event only led to increased visits to the home by civic inspectors. Muscatello eventually sold Franklin Castle to the Cleveland chief of police, Richard Hongisto. The chief and his wife lived in the house for less than a year before selling the place to George Mirceta, who owned it until 1984.

In 1984, Michael DeVinko was out for a drive one November day when he spotted Mirceta's "For Sale" sign. On a whim, he bought the house that day, charmed more by the potential of the place than its crumbling plaster and the fact that sinks, bathtubs and all but five fireplaces had been stripped from the interior. It took a decade, but after spending a million dollars, the place had been reasonably restored. In April 1999, the castle was sold again with plans for the restoration to continue. Its new owner does not know whether or not the place is haunted, but he does admit that the castle has a certain unique energy. Strange sounds and noises have been heard, and in certain spots in the house people experience emotions that are difficult to describe. Hauntings aside, the castle seems to have a life of its own, and those who walk through its interior can't help but feel a connection to the place. Past owners had attempted to transform the home into a restaurant, a church and an apartment building, but failed because of reported ghostly occurrences.

The castle's new owner is dedicated to continuing the restoration. A fire in November 1999 nearly destroyed the entire place, rendering plans much more complicated and expensive. But the work continues. Once completed, the home will be open again to the public and Franklin Castle can once again come to life.

Kelton House

In 1833, a young man headed out from Vermont, eager to seek his fortunes in the Midwest. He settled in Columbus, Ohio, and began working for John Stone. Within six years, the young man had become Stone's business partner and his son-in-law. At 27, Fernando Cortez Kelton had achieved success. He had a wife, Sophia, and was operating a successful wholesale dry goods and pharmaceutical firm. All Fernando needed was a home in which to raise a family and to enjoy life. Little did he know that the house he would build would eventually become an Ohio landmark and the permanent home of some Kelton family ghosts.

In 1852, Kelton House was completed, a mansion in the Greek Revival style built as the last residence on East Town Street. At the time, Town Street was just a single track dirt road, one mile east of Columbus' downtown thoroughfare, High Street. The Keltons considered their new home their place in the country. Within years, however, the once-pastoral area had developed into one of the city's finest residential neighborhoods. The Keltons counted among their neighbors Ohio's Civil War governor David Tod, and their opulent home became not just a residence, but also a meeting place where abolitionist and suffragette politics were discussed. A wealthy and distinguished family, the Keltons recognized their role in helping to guide Columbus through the turbulence of the Civil War. When Abraham Lincoln's body was carried through Columbus for viewing at Ohio State House, Fernando was one of the 14 pallbearers.

Since the Keltons' sympathies lay with the Union, their home became a stopping point along the Underground Railroad. Runaways, fugitives and free blacks all found safe

This sign outside Kelton House in Columbus reflects the family's important role in Ohio history.

harbor at Kelton House, hiding in the barn at the back of the house, in the 300-barrel cistern or in the servants' quarters. It's not known how many slaves passed through the house on their way to freedom, but strength of character need not be measured by numbers. In the face of great risk, the Keltons refused to compromise their beliefs, choosing to do all that they could do to help those who would otherwise be hunted down and prosecuted. To this end, they once took an escaped slave girl, Martha Hartway, into their home. Martha was eventually adopted as one of the family, and was later married at Kelton House.

But while Martha may have escaped the Civil War unscathed, ironically the Keltons did not. Oscar, the oldest son who only wanted to do his part for the Union cause, ended up making the ultimate sacrifice. As a member of the 95th Regiment Ohio Volunteer Infantry, Oscar had fought in

Tennessee and Kentucky, and served during the siege of Vicksburg. He was killed at the Battle of Brice's Crossroads near Guntown, Mississippi, in 1864. His death would inadvertently lead to his father's demise just two years later. While Fernando was on his way to Mississippi to reclaim his son's body, he was thrown out of his wagon when it got caught in a rut. He landed awkwardly on his head and was plagued with unrelenting dizziness and headaches. In 1866, Fernando was working in his office one day when he was stricken with dizziness. Seeking fresh air, he wandered over to his third-story office window. He lost his balance and tumbled from the building to the pavement below. He was carried back to his home where he died. Sophia survived her husband and son by 22 years.

Sophia left the house to her son Frank Kelton and his wife Belle Coit Kelton, a noted suffragette who was one of the first two women to attend Ohio State University. At some point, Frank traded homes with his older brother Edwin and his wife, Laura Bruce Kelton. They raised five daughters there: Grace, Ella, Laura, Lucy and Louise. The oldest of these girls, Grace, was the last of the Keltons to live in Kelton House. A noted interior designer who had a hand in the decoration of the Kennedy White House, Grace died on Christmas Eve at the age of 94. In her will, she stipulated that the home would be left to the Columbus Foundation and that they had six months to restore and to open the house as a museum of local history and the decorative arts. If six months elapsed, then the home would be torn down to make way for a park. Grace did not want an apartment building to stand where three generations of her family had lived.

The Junior League of Columbus came through. In 1976, the league took control of the home and raised over $500,000 dollars to restore it to its original pristine condition. If the stories are true, the spirits of both Sophia Kelton and her granddaughter, Grace Bird Kelton, were resurrected during the restoration work.

Staff and visitors alike have reported strange and unusual phenomena in Kelton House. On a 1998 audio cassette, staff recounted their experiences with the ghostly presences. One member claims to have seen Sophia herself. On her way home one day, she looked up at the house from her car. Her attention was drawn to the window of what had once been Sophia's room overlooking Town Street. There she saw a figure, a woman dressed in black. The woman thought that she had locked someone in the house. But when she went back in to let the unfortunate soul out, a thorough and exhaustive search revealed that the home was indeed empty. As she drove home that night, she couldn't quite shake the feeling that she knew the figure she had seen in the window, that there was something familiar about the apparition.

The next day, she went to the room and searched for a reasonable explanation for what she had seen. Maybe it was a trick of light or perhaps something had been silhouetted against the window pane. She found nothing. But as she walked back down the stairs, an epiphany took place. She found herself staring at a portrait of Sophia Kelton, and then realized that she was staring at the same individual she'd seen the night before. This wasn't the only such sighting.

A docent was conducting a tour of the house. The group was conversing on the second floor landing when the docent noticed a guest walk into Grace's bedroom. Nothing unusual, she thought, except that guests were supposed to enter the bedrooms in the presence of a docent. The docent went after the guest to alert her of her mistake but the room was empty.

A Kelton House staff member once saw the ghost of Sophia Kelton in one of the house's windows.

When asked about her experience, the docent responded that while she didn't see anything resembling a spirit or a ghost, she did feel something "warm and friendly in the air."

Chris Woodyard recounts how another woman decided that she could no longer work at Kelton House. When asked why, she claimed that a woman had been staring at her from Sophia's old room as she left. When she described the figure, the description, once again, matched that of Sophia Kelton. One employee at the home remembered how residents in the neighboring apartments once asked her whether or not someone lived in the home at night or if the lights in the home were set to a security timer. "I said no," recalls the employee, "and then they told me that they only asked because sometimes at night, lights in the house would go on and off."

If the lights were not on a security timer and no one stayed in the home at night, then why would lights be on at night? One day, the employee made sure to turn off all the lights before she went to her car at day's end. As she stood in the driveway, curiosity got the better of her and she turned around. She was stunned to see the light in Grace Kelton's old bedroom still on.

Grace manifests herself as cold spots and with the strong scent of perfume, but has been known to do more than just make an appearance. When staff members walk into the home and realize that furniture has been rearranged, the blame is pinned on Grace. Others working in the home constantly hear whistling and phantom footsteps. In life, Grace enjoyed a prosperous career as an interior designer, and was active in the arts and preservation communities. Even in death, it seems, Grace still feels the pull of her passions. Georgeanne Reuter, the house's current director, notes that the spirits tend to increase their activity when new employees are hired at the home. "Grace and Sophia," Reuter claims, "want to make sure that the new ones are OK. It's a big responsibility to take care of this house."

Although she has worked at Kelton House for 19 years, Georgeanne has yet to encounter the spirits. "I think I've made it clear to the spirits that I don't want to see anything," she says. "I guess that means I believe in them, but I'd rather not hear from them." The only unexplained experience Reuter had took place one night an hour after a reception, when she heard a door slam, then footsteps and then a door slamming again. "I don't know if it was a ghost or not," she says. "But if it was a guest from the reception, why would you hide for an hour?" Reuter is certain that everyone from the reception had left; her suspicions about what she heard were confirmed one evening at Kelton House. A meeting was held at the home for employees and visitors alike to share their encounters with the paranormal. When Reuter shared her story, two others reported having heard the same thing on different occasions.

Reuter hints that there may be another spirit roaming the halls of Kelton House. She describes how three volunteers were walking from the kitchen to the main staircase when the girl in the lead stopped in her tracks. Even though there was nothing in front of her but empty space, she had the distinct sensation that she had bumped into someone, someone quite tall. Standing there, puzzled, she next heard what she could only describe as the sound of someone snapping their fingers. So too did the volunteer standing behind her. The third volunteer heard and felt nothing. Reuter isn't sure who this spirit might be; being quite tall, it's unlikely the spirit is a Kelton. The Keltons were rather short.

Today, stepping into Kelton House is to travel through time—to life in the 19th century. It is impossible not to feel the weight of its history as visitors take in a grandfather clock built in 1790, brass gaseliers manufactured in 1851 or Chippendale-style mirrors with gold-leaf frames assembled in 1841. The house also features the Ohio Underground Railroad Marker, the first of its kind in the state, erected in November 1999. It serves as a testament to both the spirit of the Keltons and the struggle for freedom. In the near future, the house plans to set aside space in the basement for an

Underground Railroad learning station that will provide visitors with a journey into the past. Local third graders will enact a scene in which Martha Hartway, the adopted Kelton, first encounters the Kelton children. If Kelton House is in fact a living museum, the spirits of Sophia, Grace and whoever else still haunts the home are certainly its most interesting artifacts.

The Buxton Inn

Granville is a small, quiet town halfway between Columbus and Zanesville. After Ohio entered the Union in 1803, it became a convenient resting point—a place for weary travelers to stay for an evening or two on the Columbus–Newark route. The town's history is nowhere more apparent than in the old Buxton Inn on 313 East Broadway. Owned and operated for the last 20 years by Orville and Audrey Orr, the Buxton is one of Ohio's oldest inns—as well as a permanent home for several ghostly guests.

In 1812, a building was erected by Orrin Granger to serve as a mail delivery depot and stagecoach stop. During its incarnation as The Tavern, the structure was graced by noted individuals such as Charles Dickens, presidents Abraham Lincoln and William McKinley, Harriet Beecher Stowe and James Whitcomb Riley. Henry Ford was so enamoured of the place that he offered to buy it with hopes of dismantling the building and rebuilding it in Dearborn, Michigan. The owner refused. According to its current co-owner, Audrey Orr, a man named Major Buxton took ownership of the inn in 1865 and ran it until his death in 1905. From there, it passed through a number of owners until finally falling into the hands of Ethel Bounell, a singer and actress who ran the inn from 1934 until 1961, when she willed the building to her longtime companion, Nell Schoeller. Schoeller continued to operate the inn until 1972, always accompanied by her cat, Major Buxton, named after the previous owner. Even today, the cat still adorns the Buxton Inn's logo.

In 1972, Orrin and Audrey Orr assumed ownership of the inn. Upon arrival, the couple set out to restore the property. It promised to be a monumental task. Because the inn had suffered extensive termite damage, everything from the plumbing to the ventilation had to be improved. But the Orrs were up to the challenge; the work appealed to their love and respect for the history of the building. According to Woodyard, after the couple stripped away layers of paint from the black walnut exterior, they had the original paint analyzed. It turned out to consist of a mixture of buttermilk and crushed shells of cochineal beetles. As much as possible, the Orrs preserved the building's original colors and design. The renewed Buxton Inn opened again for business on Friday, September 13, 1974, a perfectly appropriate date considering what had occurred in the house during restoration.

The Orrs had heard the stories about the hauntings in the Buxton Inn but had not encountered anything out of the ordinary until shortly after renovations began. According to an article from the *Sunday Magazine* of the *Columbus Dispatch* from 1979, carpenters working in the inn boasted that they didn't believe in ghosts and that something extraordinary would have to happen before they did. The apparitions, it seems, were more than ready for the challenge.

The workmen usually worked long hours well into the evening. But one day, Orville Orr noticed that they were leaving earlier than usual and he asked them why. One worker

Spirits of former owners haunt the historic Buxton Inn in Granville.

sheepishly admitted that something was going on in the house. He explained that as early as 6 PM a number of them had seen a woman dressed in a blue gown open the stairway door, walk across the back balcony and back down the stairs. After that, she vanished right before their eyes, like breaths on a cold winter day.

Mr. Orr experienced the same thing early one morning. He was getting ready to leave the building and had made a thorough search to make sure that it was empty. Suddenly, the front door opened and Mr. Orr heard the distinct sound of someone walking up stairs, across the balcony and down again. He didn't see anything, but he heard the phantom footsteps. Again, he searched the building; of course it was empty. When he returned to check the front door, he found it bolted shut. Obviously frustrated and flustered, Mr. Orr called out to nothing in particular, "If you want this place, you can just have it!"

Mrs. Orr had a similar experience one night in 1973 when she was painting the kitchen walls. "I was painting," she says, "when out of my peripheral vision, I saw what looked like a man." She thought nothing of the apparition, thinking it was her husband watching her. But when she asked him later if he had been watching her, he replied that he hadn't even been in the kitchen that evening.

Mrs. Orr returned to the kitchen to resume her painting. Once again, she noticed the same form she had encountered earlier. She could see the form approaching her. He was about her height and wore dark clothes. But when Mrs. Orr turned to confront the man, "he faded out." Unsure of what was happening, Mrs. Orr said aloud, "I don't know what's going on, but it's scaring me."

Although the mysterious man—believed to be Major Buxton—has yet to reappear before Mrs. Orr, employees and guests have reported seeing a man dressed in late 19th century clothes. One particular night, Mrs. Orr was preparing for an event in the kitchen. A bartender came in and said, "Who's taking care of the man by the fireplace?" Mrs. Orr found the question odd, as she was positive no one had yet arrived for the function. She made her way to the fireplace with the bartender. When they got there, the man was gone. When she asked other employees, all claimed that they hadn't seen a man enter or leave.

Another time, according to Mrs. Orr, a young parapsychology student from Ohio State University visited the inn and swore he saw the figure of Major Buxton in the dining room. The student told the Orrs that Buxton just wanted to let the couple know that their plans to open the basement wall to make a tunnel between the front and back basement were fine. The Orrs were flabbergasted. There was no way that the student could be perpetrating a hoax. After all, only three people knew about the plans: the Orrs and an engineer who had been consulted six years earlier. He had warned them that if the wall was taken out, the whole front of the house could be lost. Obviously, Major Buxton disagreed.

"I started out as a skeptic," says Mrs. Orr when asked about the strange and unusual events. "It's my husband who's the true believer, but…a number of things have happened over the years that can't be easily discounted." According to popular legend, the Buxton Inn is haunted by at least three separate spirits: Ethel Bounell and two Major Buxtons—the man and the cat. In 1975, the Orrs inquired about ridding themselves of their permanent guests. A number of psychics walked through the halls and sensed spirits, claiming that the ghosts of the Buxton Inn were benevolent. Today, only a fear of the unknown will keep guests from enjoying the atmosphere. The phantom footsteps, spontaneously opening doors and heavy smells of Ethel Bounell's gardenia perfume are the inn's legacy brought to life.

When the Orrs first learned about the ghosts, they kept the stories private, thinking that if word got around, business would be hurt. But ever since the *Columbus Dispatch* article about the Buxton's spirited guests, the phantoms have done nothing but bring people in—people eager to experience something unusual and eerie.

Mrs. Orr says that a guest recently approached her with a story. "He had got up from bed and went to the bathroom," she says. "When he came back, his pillows were fluffed and his bed had been straightened up." Complimentary mints placed on guests' pillows have a habit of disappearing and television sets turn themselves on in the dead of night. Guests staying in room 9, Miss Schoeller's old private residence, claim they feel the presence of something on their bed, something similar to a cat. The presence is probably Major Buxton, reclining luxuriously in the Victorian-style room.

Under the Orrs, the Buxton Inn has grown into a complex of five buildings, each one lovingly and painstakingly restored to its Victorian splendor. But none haunts the imagination more fully than the main building at 313 East Broadway.

3
Wandering Women

~

We often wonder about our mortality. What happens after death? What will our legacy be? How will we be remembered? Can we attain immortality? For some individuals, death is only the first step in a completely new life. Take, for example, the wandering women in this chapter, who spend an eternity revisiting the scenes of their deaths. For some, lost love occasions repeated visits among the living; for others, a special connection to a place or person inspires them to return. Regardless of their reasons, these women have transcended mortality through death. Their spirits ensure that people do not forget about their legacies or the impact they had upon the lives they touched.

~

The Victoria Theatre

The mystery continues to confound people even today, years after the incident was supposed to have taken place. It might even have faded from memory were it not for the unwillingness of one particular actress to quit the earthly stage.

Sometime in the late 19th century, an actress went into her dressing room to change into a black taffeta dress. When she emerged, she realized that she had forgotten a key prop, a fan. She walked back down the stairway to her room and smiled politely at the security guard. He, in turn, watched her walk into her dressing room and shut the door behind her. As her stage cue came and went, the actress remained in her dressing room. The stage manager, irate and frustrated, pounded down the steps to her dressing room, demanding to know why one of his players had seen fit to ruin his show. There was no response. Finally, the manager and the guard forced open the door; after a thorough search of the room, they found it empty. The actress had disappeared.

How? It's not clear. There were only two ways out of the dressing room. One was past the security guard on the staircase. The other was through a window three stories above the ground. The guard never saw the actress pass by him after she went into her room to retrieve the forgotten fan, leaving only the window as her only possible exit. Regardless, the actress was never seen again, at least not physically. And yet she has never really left the historic Victoria Theatre in Dayton, Ohio. In fact, her spirit is now almost as old as the Second Empire building itself.

Restored in 1988 by the Arts Center Foundation for a fee of $17.5 million, the auditorium seats 1200. If the long-lost actress makes one of her now-famous, not altogether unexpected appearances, the audience might witness more than a typical performance. Although the actress has been missing since the late 19th century and has probably been dead for many years, she continues to adore the stage. Ever since her mysterious disappearance, patrons and employees alike have detected the scent of roses as she brushes by people walking up or down the staircase. In an interview with ghost writer Barbara Smith, David Hastings of the Victoria Theatre claims that "you can hear the rustling of her gown as she moves through the theatre. It's not only happened to me, it's happened to a lot of the employees here and even to a lot of the patrons."

While some fear the paranormal and avoid the unusual, it seems as if the ghost of the Victoria Theatre has not lost any of her charms over the years. When Hastings first came to the theater in 1975, he didn't believe in ghosts. "I knew it was all hogwash," he says. "But as I was leaving the theatre around 10:00 one night, I heard footsteps on the stage. I thought it was our technical director, so I called out…there wasn't any answer and the steps continued." Technical director John Renzel later told Hastings that he'd heard the ghost, to which Hastings replied, "Oh bullwinkle." But soon enough, the bullwinkle became too much to ignore. The ghost began to make her presence felt and soon enough Hastings was embracing the actress as "positive energy and a positive influence…a friend of the theater." But from 1988 to 1990, Hastings feared that the ghost had left the building during renovations.

Just before the theatre was closed for its renovations, Kelly Franz, the marketing director, compiled a slide show—a tribute of sorts to the Victoria's past. Each night, after sorting out the slides on a light table, Franz would leave and lock

A phantom actress who disappeared more than a hundred years ago still trods the boards at the Victoria Theatre.

her office. Every morning for the next four days, she would return, only to find her slides rearranged. Of course, Franz would change them back only to find the slides out of order again. Finally, Franz lost her patience and left the slides in the order she found them. The slides remained undisturbed after that—that is, until the slide presentation was actually underway. Two projectors alternated back and forth between slides until one just stopped functioning suddenly, even though it had power and a bulb. The glitch was attributed to the spirit and her apparent dislike for the proposed renovations. It wasn't until work was underway and the spirit began playing practical jokes and pranks on the construction workers that Hastings was able to breathe a sigh of relief. The spirit was going to stay.

Three or four years ago, a local television station, WDTN, came to the theater to do a story on haunted places. During his interview, Hastings watched the reporter, Martha Dunsky, abruptly walk over to the staircase leading to the balcony. After she returned to finish the interview, Hastings asked her what was so intriguing. She claimed to have heard the rustling of the actress' taffeta dress, and thought she might have captured the sound on tape through the boom microphone being used for the interview. Dunsky hadn't been gone for a half hour before she called Hastings, ecstatic. She had, indeed, managed to record the rustling of the Victoria spirit.

Laura Januzzi has been working at the Victoria Theatre as a media and public relations coordinator since September 2001. She has yet to experience anything strange or unusual but does believe in the presence of an energy or a ghost. "I'm aware of her presence for sure," Januzzi says.

Henry House
and the Apple Lady

In the 1830s, a professional carpenter bought 125 acres of land in what is now the Cleveland suburb of Parma Heights. Robert Warner Henry also wanted to be a farmer, but he wasn't about to strand his wife, Frances, in the wilderness. A two-story, white-pillared home was soon erected for her, and by all accounts life on the farm was happy indeed. As the couple's twelve children grew up and began families of their own, Henry House, as it was fondly christened, never lacked for warmth; the place was always thronging with individuals of all ages. Some were in-laws, while others were relatives who just needed a little time to get back on their feet. Whatever their situations, they were all welcome. It's been reported that Henry House also sheltered runaway slaves who sought the freedom promised to them at the end of the Underground Railroad.

On one snowy December night in 1863, Frances Henry got in her carriage, seeking solitude in the absence of any communication from her son Fitzroy, who had left to fight in the Civil War months before and who had not been heard from since. She directed her horse to take her through her favorite apple orchard and further into the open pasture beyond. She wanted to escape her thoughts and fears about her son, but sitting there in the carriage, Frances couldn't help but notice that there was something trapped in the deep folds of her dress. As she opened her knees to see exactly what it was, there was a flash of white as something tumbled down onto the carriage floor. Squinting down onto the floor, Frances saw a single white rose lying at her feet. Her heart became heavy with grief; in that white rose, she saw death. She returned home and handed the flower to her husband with the words, "Fitty is dead." Three weeks later, news arrived from the front that Fitzroy Harrison Henry had been killed in the Battle of Chickamauga. Frances Henry, a spiritualist, had intuited the death of her own son.

Frances Henry died in 1880 when she was hit by a train while walking along the tracks near her home. Strangely enough, her body bore no marks; there was not even the hint of a bruise to suggest at what had occurred. Stranger still was what took place when her body was laid out to rest in the north wing of Henry House. Throughout the night, a loud rumbling noise kept coming from the room in which Frances lay—the sound, it was believed, of her settling in.

Frances Henry appears to have settled in indefinitely. In 1995, her great-great-grandson, William Troy, wrote of his experiences with his long-dead relative in *Cleveland Magazine*. While a self-proclaimed skeptic when it comes to the eerie and the supernatural, Troy became receptive to the inexplicable on the basis of Frances Henry's story.

As a child, Troy heard numerous stories about Frances and Henry House but never actually saw the home until he was 13. Early in the 20th century, the home had passed out of the family's hands, and it wasn't until one Sunday afternoon in November that Troy finally saw a home that had previously only existed in his imagination. Stepping out of the car with his mother and grandmother, Troy made his way to the front of the house. They rang the bell and were promptly greeted by a couple who invited the family inside when they learned of their identities. The wife was eager to learn of everything that had happened in the home. Before Troy's grandmother could even begin, however, she was interrupted by the wife, who said that she had had the most difficult time keeping a maid employed in the home. They complained about finding beds they had only made up an hour ago rumpled and mussed, and how they couldn't get a pot of water to come to a boil on the stove. Someone or something was always turning the heat off. Troy's grandmother nodded her head in fond recognition. She told the couple they had nothing to worry about, that her grandmother had been a merry prankster and meant no harm. At the time, the 13-year-old Troy wanted nothing more than to get out of Henry House.

Two decades passed before he returned to Henry House. He was interviewing a candidate for a job and, when he asked her to name her previous places of employment, she mentioned the Parma Heights City Hall. Following up, he asked for the city hall's phone number and address. She claimed that the offices had recently moved, that the switch had taken place because the old building was a unusual place to work in. Files would disappear on their own, only to turn up days or even weeks later in places completely unexpected. She described the place as an "old, old house with lots of little rooms and beautiful two-story white pillars on the front." The prospective employee had just described Henry House perfectly.

By 1995, the house had become a beauty salon. When Troy drove by it once, he decided to stop by briefly, spurred on by curiosity and nostalgia. He made his introductions and secured permission to walk the building on the strength of his position as great-great-grandson of its original inhabitants. Although he never once mentioned anything about the hauntings that might have taken place inside Henry House, a manicurist had asked him to talk about the Apple Lady as he was readying to leave. Troy had never heard of the Apple

Lady before but had a pretty good idea who she was. Troy ended up staying at the salon for the better part of an hour as he heard excited accounts of doors rapidly opening and closing, of toilets operating on their own, of empty rooms being locked from the inside and of people starting conversations with nothingness. Most prominent of all, the frequent and powerful odor of apples. Frances Henry, after all, did so love her apple orchards. Troy was pleased with the salon's unwavering belief in the Apple Lady's happiness. Initially, the staff had considered an exorcism to rid the house of the spirit, but soon realized that the Apple Lady meant no harm. They, after all, were the intruders and the spirit had a right to stay in the home as long as possible.

Although Troy continues to question whether or not his ancestor really is a permanent resident of Henry House, a part of him longs to believe in Frances. He does not deny the impact the ghost has had on those who have lived in the home, and is thankful that she continues to have friends. He writes in *Cleveland Magazine* that the next time he returns to Henry House, he plans to "bring along a single white rose, to let Frances know that others share in her loves and sorrows."

Squire's Castle

The North Chagrin Reservation is a 1912-acre wilderness preserve outside of Cleveland—one jewel in a string of 13 others encircling the city, creating what is fondly referred to as the Emerald Necklace. Established by Cleveland Metroparks in 1917, the 14 reservations, all connected by parkways, cover nearly 20,000 acres of varying landscapes and provide Clevelanders with a place to escape from the city.

The North Chagrin Reservation contains some of the finest examples of original natural vegetation in Cuyahoga County. Stands of beech, sugar maple and hemlock are still abundant, and the particularly observant can also find red maple, tulip, ash, cucumber and tupelo. Wildflowers are plentiful, with hepatica, spring beauty and white trillium flourishing in great numbers. The reservation is also home to the oldest remaining stand of white pines in the Cleveland Metroparks, a rarity considering that the pines were the tree of choice for shipbuilders during the 19th century. Little wonder, then, that when Cleveland businessman Feargus B. Squire decided to use his wealth to create a hunting paradise on earth, he amassed over 500 acres in what would eventually become the North Chagrin Reservation. There, he could hunt deer and wild turkeys to his heart's content. But as it is with the best laid plans, Squire's dreams never quite became a reality.

In true American fashion, Squire came from humble origins. Through shrewdness, cunning and steel will, he became vice-president of Standard Oil after partnering with John D. Rockefeller's early oil businesses in Cleveland. He and his wife Rebecca settled into a comfortable life in the city. Despite all he'd accumulated, though, something was missing from Squire's life in Cleveland. An avid hunter, he lamented the lack of opportunities to indulge his hobby in Cleveland. He then decided that he would build his own summer retreat, creating a hunting ground and erecting a grand hunting lodge. In Cuyahoga County, he found exactly what he was looking for and began buying acres of land.

Finally, in 1890, using stone quarried on his property, Squire began construction on a gate house, the first structure that would sit at the entrance to a grand estate. Unfortunately, he neglected to consider how his decision to live in the country for four months of the year might affect Rebecca. She might have been a wonderful wife and mother, but most of all Rebecca was a socialite, relishing high society and everything her position and privilege had to offer. Nature, for her, held nothing; she saw in the woods and wilderness not the nostalgic simplicity of Wordsworth's Tintern Abbey, but the chaotic savagery of the Augustans. She resisted the move as much as possible, staying at her home in Cleveland whenever Squire watched over construction on the property. Nobody knows for certain why Rebecca decided to accompany her husband to the country one summer, but she did.

Her time there was far from happy. She couldn't bear to think of spending summers at the property. Legends claim that she developed insomnia and took to wandering the gatehouse and the grounds until late at night carrying a red lantern to light her way. One evening, she made her way to the basement of the gatehouse, which Squire had turned into a trophy room, complete with the stuffed heads of the many animals he'd shot and killed on countless hunting expeditions. Various traps and snares rounded out the decor. Nobody knows exactly what she saw while down there, but the stuffed heads must have appeared quite shocking in the grim half-light and shadows of the lantern. Something terrified Rebecca and she attempted to flee from the room. In her haste, she tripped and fell awkwardly. Some say she broke her neck, while others believe she fell into one of the many snares hanging from the ceiling and slowly suffocated. When Squire discovered what had happened, he was apparently so distraught that he abandoned his plans for the grand estate in the wilderness and left for Cleveland, never to return to the site. His gatehouse became known as Squire's Castle, a tragically ironic moniker.

In 1922, Squire sold off his estate to developers; only later was it used for park development. As for his dream, the gatehouse still stands, although not with its original splendor. All that remains, in fact, is just the outer shell. But something intangible has survived—Rebecca's spirit. It seems that she has been forced to walk the halls and woods she hated in life for an eternity in death. People have reported seeing the ghostly glow of her red lantern cutting its way through the darkness in a neverending struggle with her insomnia. The light is sometimes accompanied by the screams of Rebecca falling to her death.

But is it really the ghost of Rebecca haunting the land around Squire's Castle? Squire's wife, after all, didn't die of a gruesome fall; rather, she died from a stroke in 1929, quite some time after Squire had sold his property and far away from the reservation. Still, it is very possible that her spirit lingers in a place that occasioned such sorrow in her life. Park employees still hear reports even now, especially at Halloween, that a light can be seen moving back and forth within the remains of Squire's Castle. Is it Rebecca? No one seems to know for certain. Squire's Castle may have remained just a dream for the man who built it, but it now haunts the dreams of those who visit it.

The Taft Museum

She has a way of helping people believe.

The chief of security at the Taft Museum, John Ring, can still recall the moment he cast skepticism aside and began to believe. He told his story to Derek Krewedl of the newspaper *The Downtowner* in October 2001. Ring's moment of epiphany came in the late 1970s. He was watching over a chamber music concert when he was approached by several guests, each with the same complaint—they were distracted by the sound of a crying baby just in the background, somewhere outside the music room. Ring set off to investigate. But even after an exhaustive and thorough search of the building's other rooms and hallways, no baby was ever found. In fact, after questioning other employees about the incident, Ring learned that a baby hadn't even been in the building that day. He remembered that when he first began his job, he had been regaled with eerie stories by other security officers—stories of strange cries and footsteps in empty places.

But it wasn't until she entered the picture that Ring understood fully what he'd been told. As he was walking down the long hallway just outside the concert room, Ring heard footsteps behind him and then his name called out in a woman's voice. He turned around to respond but there was nothing there. She had called out to him, and he was converted. Annie had shown him the possibilities and now, every time Ring passes by her portrait in the music room, he is careful to wish Mrs. Taft a good morning.

Annie Taft died in 1931 and her home and its collection of art, so lovingly and painstakingly created over many years with her husband, passed to the people of Cincinnati.

The elegant Taft Museum in Cincinnati, where the ghost of Anna Taft still shows her appreciation for the arts

The house, built by merchant Martin Baum in 1820, now stands as the Taft Museum, where the Tafts' collections of European paintings and Chinese porcelains are displayed.

Baum constructed the large Federal-style house on a lot on the eastern edge of Cincinnati but didn't live there long, as the bank panic of 1820 devastated him financially and he was forced to move. The grand building was then used as an all-girls school until 1829, when it was bought by one of Cincinnati's wealthiest citizens, Nicholas Longworth.

A patron of the arts, Longworth commissioned artist Robert Scott Duncanson to paint eight murals on the house's walls, works that launched Duncanson's career and established a legacy of arts support within the home that continued when David Sinton bought the home in 1871. While the murals are now seen as trademarks of the Taft home, the Tafts themselves never saw them. It wasn't until the home was being transformed into a museum that layers and layers of wallpaper were stripped away to reveal the stunning river and landscape scenes.

Sinton lived in the home with his daughter, Anna, and her husband, Charles Phelps Taft, the older half-brother of former president William Howard Taft and publisher of the *Cincinnati Times-Star*. The two were married in the music room upstairs in 1873, and when Anna's father died in 1890, her inheritance made her the richest woman in Ohio, a position allowing her and husband to pursue their love of the arts. Between 1902 and 1927, the two amassed what Jane Durrell called, on the 60th anniversary of the Taft Museum, a "coherent and harmonious collection, a first-class collection of art."

Charles passed away in 1929; Anna followed in 1931. The house, along with its art collection, was willed to the city of Cincinnati. In death, the Tafts passed on the pleasure they felt while gazing upon their collected works of art. But it seems that the Tafts themselves might still be enjoying their home and their life's work, even in death.

Staff maintain that there are spirits roaming the halls of the Taft Museum. History, after all, has had time to foster the development of a number of them. David Sinton, his daughter and her husband, for example, all died in the home. The daughter, Anna, remains the best known spirit.

She is said to be a friendly, if mischievous, spirit, fond of interacting with staff and patrons. Owen Findsen, a reporter for the *Cincinnati Enquirer,* recorded an account by John Ring from Halloween 1995. Ring indicated that he was working in the garden when he noticed two ladies leaving the museum in a bit of a hurry. Apparently, the mother and daughter had been in the parlor looking at a painting. The mother claimed that someone had tapped on her shoulder, only when she turned, no one was there. The two decided to leave the place quickly. Anna's overtures were not welcome at the time.

Anna once appeared to a girl waiting for her boyfriend, who was a security guard at the museum. Standing outside, the girl waved at a figure standing at a second-floor window, thinking it was her boyfriend. The figure did not wave back. When the boyfriend finally finished his shift and got into the girl's car, she asked him why he hadn't waved back at her. He claimed that he had been in the basement and hadn't been upstairs at all. The second floor, moreover, had been locked down; any movement there would have set off motion sensors.

In the gift shop, books fall off shelves, only to land, every time, five feet away, face up. In a downstairs office with only one entrance, employees return only to find that someone or something has wedged a chair underneath the doorknob—not outside, but inside the office. One time, several stacks of heavy books were placed in front of the door after it was locked; when people returned to work the next morning, they cleared away the books, only to find that their attempt to thwart the supernatural had failed. Upstairs, the attic has many unexplained cold spots, and more than one worker has reported feeling that someone was blocking his or her way into an attic hallway. Who is responsible for all these events isn't exactly clear; it may be Anna or any of the other spirits in the Taft Museum. There are times, however, when there can be no debate.

Even in death, Anna has not lost her passion for the arts. Katie Laur was playing country music in the garden one day when a gift shop customer, Treva Lambing, noticed that a security camera at the back of the museum seemed to be malfunctioning. Instead of panning across the grounds as it was supposed to do, the camera was pointing straight down at the ground. Lambing went over to make a report to a security guard on duty at the time. But when she reached the guard, Lambing noticed that she was staring up at the balcony. So she looked up too. There on the balcony was the figure of a woman in a long, pink gown, her feet tapping to the beat of the music. The way she looked—combined with the fact that there is no door to the balcony—convinced the onlookers that she was the spirit of Anna, taking time to enjoy the music in the sweet perfumed air of the garden.

Anna is so prominent, in fact, that Ring makes sure all the new employees meet and greet her portrait. Tamera Muente was thus initiated when she started working at the Taft Museum in late 2001. Despite the introduction, Muente "is still waiting patiently to meet Annie." She may have to wait a while. The museum is currently closed, undergoing major renovations. The changes may very well drive away the spirit, but one should hope that Anna stays, for she is perhaps the most valuable specimen in a house full of priceless objects.

Esther Hale

For most people, August 12 isn't a date to note on the calendar. But for one particular individual, the day marked a lost life, a broken heart and the beginning of the end. Dead for years now, Esther Hale is a spirit with a soul divided by fate. She lives in a world of shadows and fosters a long-festering resentment towards life and the promise of happiness.

Early in the nineteenth century, canals were built in the new state of Ohio as a means of opening up trade routes between the western markets and the more lucrative eastern ones. The network of canals caused a boom in local economies as towns sprung up along the waterways in rapid succession to take advantage of the new financial opportunities. Fortunes were made and fortunes were lost; the heady times could not last, though. The train soon replaced the canal network and the boom of the nineteenth century winked out. By the late 1880s, the dream was over. The only monuments to mark the past were rotting timbers and decrepit buildings. An entire way of life had suffered the same fate as Esther Hale had so many years before.

The area that briefly flourished with the prosperity of the canal is known as Beaver Creek State Parks. The past is writ large in both abandoned towns and haunted spirits. Near East Liverpool, there is little left to mark a town called Sprucevale except two run-down buildings. Only accessible by foot or horse, the town never devoted a monument to its most famous denizen, Esther Hale, who is reported to walk the bridge crossing over Beaver Creek every August 12. There is no need for a memorial because she has become her very own monument.

In August 1837, Esther Hale was simply another young woman whose dreams, though simple, were her entire world.

All she wanted was to spend the rest of her life in wedded bliss with her one and only. Although no record of her beloved survives, it is clear that Esther's hopes met a crushing end.

On August 12, Esther woke to a beautiful summer morning. While she was normally inclined to stay in bed for a little longer before beginning a new day, today was an exception. She practically jumped out of bed, unable to contain her excitement. The wedding dress hung from the closet door, and the beautiful bride-to-be was soon dressed in shimmering white. She quivered with excitement as the months of anticipation converged into one single glorious day. From that day onward, she would be a wife and, some day soon, a mother as well.

But hours after the appointed time, Esther was still unwed. She continued to wait, even as the hum of speculation and curiosity filled the chapel. The groom never showed. And it wasn't until the chapel was nearly empty that Esther faced the truth. No one knows why, but Esther would never marry. Some claim that her groom abandoned her, never to be heard from again. Others are somewhat more forgiving and believe that he had been killed the night before in an unfortunate accident. Regardless of why she had been abandoned, Esther was never able to recover from her loss.

After she returned from the chapel that night, Esther turned her back on life as well. Days passed, yet no one had seen or heard from Esther. Concerned friends visited her home, only to find that she was still in her wedding dress; worse, the home was still decorated for a wedding reception. After refusing all pleas to come outside or change clothes, Esther submitted when her friends begged her at least to eat something. She then asked her friends to leave. They did and Esther was alone once again. This pattern continued for weeks. Try as they might, Esther's friends could not save her from the darkness of her soul. Esther was still breathing but her vacant eyes revealed that she was forever lost.

In December, a delivery boy noticed that snowdrifts had piled in and around her doorway. The door itself was open and snow was creeping across the floor. The delivery boy raced to tell the sheriff. When he arrived to investigate, he found Esther's body slumped over the kitchen table. The coroner guessed that she had been dead for several weeks.

Esther Hale was buried in a site long forgotten, apparently still wearing her wedding dress. Motorists and pedestrians crossing the Beaver Creek Bridge on August 12 have reported seeing the decaying figure of a woman in a frayed white wedding dress—a kind of martyr to unrequited love and faded hopes. Esther's ghost has been known to lunge at passersby. Legend states that if she touches you, you will wither and die as she recovers her youth, feeding off the life force of those who share the high hopes she once had.

4
Cemeteries

~

Many gravestones are inscribed with the words "Rest in Peace." But judging by the amount of supernatural activity reported in cemeteries, very few spirits take these words to heart. To walk through any cemetery is to walk through history; to walk through a haunted cemetery is a different matter altogether. In a haunted cemetery, the past has taken root and flourished, issuing forth a chorus of ghostly voices. Lean in and you can hear the fading whispers of the lonely dreamer, the tortured soul or the broken-hearted. These are the voices of the dead, reminding us not to forget their brief stays on earth.

~

The Bauer Farmhouse

Most people want to believe that a home they move into can become theirs. Sometimes that just isn't the case, and the weight of history overwhelms those who are just trying to survive the present. But as much as one might try, the ghosts of the past can't be ignored. One Ohio couple couldn't enjoy their future together until they reckoned with the unusual history of their long-abandoned farmhouse.

The Bauer Farmhouse in Clermont County sits in the northern part of Owensville Village. When first erected by the Bauers, it was deemed a grand home, complete with a verandah that wrapped around three sides of the house. The Bauers lived there happily for years until their deaths. A family then moved in before abandoning the home to a schoolteacher, Emily, and her long-suffering boyfriend, Billy.

When Emily agreed to marry, after months of debate and waiting, the two celebrated their impending nuptials by buying the vacated farm. As a present of sorts to his future bride, Billy spent long hours renovating the aging farmhouse in an attempt to transform the structure into a home. Soon enough, the two moved in and settled into what they hoped would be a peaceful and fulfilling existence out in the country. But it wasn't to be.

Right from the start, life on the farm was anything but idyllic. While Billy slept heavily, Emily would wake up with a start at any unusual sounds. Naturally, Billy would then be roused from his slumber to reassure his wife that the sounds were not menacing. In the new home, Emily found sleeping through the night impossible. A strange scratching sound from the front of the house kept her guessing as to its source. Billy tried to calm her down, telling her that homes all have their own unique sounds, and that their farmhouse was no exception. Billy suspected that field mice or some other rodents under the porch were responsible for keeping his wife up at night.

Yet, search as he did, he could never track down the source of the sounds. An examination of the home's underbelly only turned up several jugs of wine, now vinegar, and the rusting remains of what was once a bicycle. To ensure that he didn't miss anything, Billy installed a porch light and bought a host of guard animals to deter any unwelcome guests. But despite the precautions, the scratching continued.

One evening, events occured that would bring about a resolution to this particularly persistent problem. As usual, Emily was roused from slumber by the scratching, but this time it suddenly stopped and was replaced by the sounds of footsteps that made their way to the bedroom. Billy got up and pressed his ear to the door; he heard the steps stop right outside. Convinced that someone or something was out there, Billy loaded his shotgun and courageously threw open the door. He found himself staring down an empty hallway, with his terrier whimpering and cowering in the darkness. Emily finally told Billy what she had suspected for so long— their home was haunted.

Billy found the idea a little preposterous but was willing to consider the hypothesis. Still, he hunkered down in the front room with his loaded shotgun trained on the front door, ready to surprise any intruder. His anxiety and concern quickly gave way to an overwhelming desire to sleep. Soon enough, Billy had fallen asleep, only to be awakened by the screams of his wife. He awoke, wondering how an intruder could have slipped past his tightly patrolled perimeter; he then realized one could have easily gotten into the home through the bedroom window.

Bursting into the bedroom, Billy found Emily alone, screaming, it turned out, from a nightmare that involved a girl stooping over something. The vision reminded Emily too much of her mother's death just a year before. Billy searched the home and yard, but could find no sign of an intruder. All he could do was resume his vigil and beat back the idea that his wife might be going slightly mad.

The next day, Billy decided to keep the farm but to move to Emily's sister's house in the village. Emily refused, claiming that things would get better, that all they needed was time. Billy consented. By nightfall, the couple were already discussing further plans for the home. Emily wanted to create a path to the back of the house, one made of flagstones as smooth as the ones at the base of their front porch steps.

Curious to see where the flagstones might have been made, Billy pried one out from the ground and turned it over. Even though the face was covered with dirt and grime from years past, he could see that there was something unusual about this flagstone. Wiping away the mud, Billy found himself staring at one half of a tombstone. Emily looked at their find, suddenly unable to get the vision from her nightmare out of her head. The nightmare had been a message, leading Emily to implore her husband to dig up all the stones in the path. When a second stone was turned over and placed next to the first, they found that the two were actually halves of a whole. The restored tombstone revealed the name Carrie Bauer, who lived from 1873 to 1897. More stones were unearthed, and by the time Billy was finished he had six stones, comprising what looked like two more tombstones. The final and sixth one was complete on its own, a tiny marker made for a child.

The recovered tombstones were carried to the graveyard just inside the pasture fence. Emily searched for graves amidst the overgrown weeds and grass. Night halted her search. The new day called for new tactics; Billy brought in a sickle and chopped at the brush until he found what he thought were seven grave markers. Underneath lay the bodies of those who had had their graves desecrated through the removal of their tombstones. Instead of honoring the dead, someone had chosen to walk on them. Billy and Emily replaced the tombstones, and as they drove the last into the ground, Clermont County experienced its first snow of the year.

The wind was fierce that night, howling its way across the land. By nightfall the next day, the storm had subsided, the air was still and the land was tucked under a comforting blanket of snow. The incessant scratchings stopped, and Emily experienced a blissful night's sleep for the first time in a long while. While Billy remained skeptical, Emily was convinced the scratching had been a plea for help from beyond the grave. Carrie Bauer, still mournful that her family's plots had been disturbed, had called out. Emily had answered. Billy was sure that the scratching would begin again once warm weather returned. He believed that the animals responsible for the scratching had simply gone into hibernation.

But when spring returned and the snow receded, the couple never again heard the scratching at their door. Billy retained his skepticism about the whole incident, but as Emily looked at the well-groomed lawn of the graveyard and its tombstones, she knew otherwise.

Athens' Paranormal History

Settlers first traveled up the Hocking River into what would become the city of Athens in 1787. To draw more people to the area, Ohio University was chartered in 1804, and the hope was that the townships of Athens and Alexander, set aside as college lands, would infuse the fledgling school with the funds necessary to maintain its existence. Of course, there was a great gap between expectation and reality; settlers were reluctant to pay their rent, and the university suffered through years marked by uncertainty and doubt. But the institution persevered, soldiering on through lean years as enrollment continued to grow.

By 1811, Athens had become a village. It was a county seat, but its relative isolation from other commercial markets slowed its growth to an imperceptible crawl. As an agricultural marketing center, Athens depended upon exports of surplus corn, wheat and smoked pork. The routes these goods took down the Hocking, Ohio and Mississippi Rivers were slow and unreliable at best. Even the completion of the Hocking Canal in 1843 did little to alleviate the situation; while its construction provided a more efficient and cost-effective route, winter's breath froze the canal and it lay vulnerable in warmer weather to flooding. It wasn't until the railroad came to Athens in 1857 that access to the eastern commercial markets became sure and reliable. In 1850, only 881 people called Athens home. By 1870, 1600 people populated the village, drawn in by the new Columbus and Hocking Valley Railroad. But while some had been drawn to Athens by its economic prospects, others sought out the relative isolation of the area for reasons altogether different. Spiritual, and not economic, fulfillment was the key. This small and unique class of individuals had been flocking to Athens as early as the beginning of the 19th century.

In 1973, Sandy Speidel wrote in *Athens Magazine* that Athens was seen by the spiritually inclined as a safe harbor—a tract of land highly receptive to spirits, continuing a trend that had begun with the land's original Indian inhabitants. Over time, Athens has suffered little in the way of natural disasters, avoiding the mass floodings and tornadoes that have ravaged other areas of southern Ohio. Its rugged terrain and proximity to water have allegedly created the right balance of positive and negative charges of ionization for spirit-life. Moreover, the children of the Appalachian, typically blessed with psychic abilities and open-minded parents, also allow a fantasy life to flourish in Athens. Those who came to Athens believing it was a spiritual zone found themselves drawn to Mount Nebo, reputedly the highest point in Athens County.

Mount Nebo was a remnant of a simpler time, an age that faded into the past as white settlers spread across the land and displaced long-standing traditions and cultures. Nebo was a mound constructed by Indians, and it was considered sacred. Hunting was forbidden there, and tribal funerals were once held there. Early in the 19th century, covens of Athens County congregated around Nebo as a center of spirituality for black and white magic cults. The witches prospered until the 1850s when they began losing ground to the rising spiritualists. To the white settlers striving to be closer to divinity, Mount Nebo was the point where they believed they could form the closest link with God.

Sometime in the 1850s, Jonathon Koons was out on a walk one evening when he felt something come over his consciousness. He heard voices speaking to him but knew not from where they came. They still spoke to him, and he felt as if he were in a trance, with his being held in sway by forces unknown. Koons believed the spirits had the following message for him. All eight of his children had great powers. If they used their talents properly, they would all go on to become great mediums, through whom the spirits could communicate with the living. Koons was also told to ascend Mount Nebo, which was his property at the time, and, like God directing Noah, was instructed to construct a special séance room to fill with all sorts of musical instruments. The finished room measured 16 feet by 12 feet and was decorated with bells hanging from the ceiling and copper plating cut into the shape of birds. It would become Koons' spiritual headquarters.

Séances were conducted regularly, each beginning with Koons playing a selection of hymns on his violin. His playing summoned other instruments to join in, and as the music of the spiritual orchestra washed over a rapt audience, it is said that phosphorous paper would float through the air. So too would a tambourine, creating a powerful breeze. At times, hands could be seen holding the paper, but that was all. Arms were never seen. The number of dead communicating with the living was set at 165; these ethereal beings passed their messages by either writing them on a blackboard or on the backs of people's heads and on their foreheads. There is also an account of a time when a spirit was writing a message on the hand of a man when the man, growing impatient, asked the spirit why it was taking so long. In response, the spirit proceeded to produce a page and a half of writing in the blink of an eye, most of which consisted of intricate drawings. The paper was folded three times and then placed on the man's lap.

In 1870, documents from the archives of Ohio University Library showed that five acres of land on Mount Nebo were purchased for $250 by Eli Curtis. Curtis and his followers came to found a kingdom on the hill, guided by the spiritualist Wilhelm Reich, who predicted that Athens would rise as the rest of the world fell.

Curtis, a member of the Morning Star Community, dedicated his purchase "to the Land of Hosts...to be used expressly for spiritual purposes and for a place to form a nucleus around which the City of the New Jerusalem is to be builded [sic] in time." The community's executive committee, divined allegedly by the spirit of Jesus of Nazareth, consisted of Curtis, William D. Hall and Chauncey Barnes. Although blessed by the spirit of Jesus of Nazareth, the members of the Morning Star Community failed in their quest. Funds dried up during the construction of a great tabernacle. By 1875, the Morning Star Community was no more, since its most active member, Barnes, decided to leave the country. In 1893, what was left of the tabernacle was torn down and removed, but there are still signs of the community that once lived on the hill.

The failures of Koons and Curtis to establish private utopias might have had something to do with the fact that Mount Nebo is not the highest point in Athens County. At 1053 feet, that distinction belongs to a point on Hooper Ridge, near County Roads 37, 36 and close to 99. Yet their presence at Mount Nebo is still apparent. Knolls with rings of white oak trees are still visible around the area, while circles of grass or rocks are common. Though only reminders of attempts to form either a spiritualist community or to found a New Jerusalem, the remnants are powerful symbols nonetheless. And while the spiritualists may not have found exactly what they were looking for, their instincts were quite correct.

Athens, after all, has been ranked by the British Society for Physical Research as one of the most haunted places on earth, and it certainly appears to be an area in harmony with the activities of the seemingly undead. Spiritualists and witches aside, the people of Athens today find that their city is the subject of numerous accounts for which there are no logical or rational explanations.

One of the more popular accounts centers on the death of an Ohio University student, David Tischman, in April 1970. In Hanning Cemetery, located in Peach Ridge, a séance was held in an attempt to contact his spirit. Equipment used included a Ouija board and two black candles. The indicator on the board didn't move once but wax from the candles dripped onto the board and pooled into the shapes of letters. It read DAVT4. To those conducting the séance, David Tischman had indeed made contact, but what did the 4 represent? It didn't take long to make the connection that Tischman had died in April, the fourth month of the year. Simms Cemetery, another one in Peach Ridge, is believed to be haunted because John Simms had been the official in charge of hanging criminals. It's believed his victims are still out there, attempting to exact revenge for what they perceive to be unjust deaths. Simms himself apparently still wanders the ground, coming out at twilight decked out in a hooded robe.

Other cemeteries in Athens are venues for the strange and unusual. On West State Street, there is a statue "dedicated to the sacred memory of the unknown dead who rest here 1806–1924." The West State Cemetery is one of the oldest in Athens, and the statue, carved in the shape of an angel, watches over those buried in unmarked graves. Her silent vigil invokes the memory of soldiers who sacrificed their

Athens' cemeteries have long been associated with the paranormal and the occult.

lives in defense of their beliefs, their culture and their customs. Known as the "crying angel," the stone angel will, on occasion, flutter her wings, as residents of Athens have reported. Peer into her face and you might observe tears trickling down her cheeks as the angel weeps for the fallen. Some claim that the angel was built as a memorial to a child who died much too young, and that the statue weeps on the child's birthday.

Bethel Cemetery also has its share of mystery. A group of a dozen graves has heads facing north, a departure from normal custom in which the graves face east so that the dead face the rising sun. Naturally, it is curious that just a dozen in this cemetery break from tradition. Folklorists and researchers offer the explanation that these people were perhaps once witches (practitioners of black and white magic), a hypothesis based on the belief that the witch heaven of Summerland lies towards the north.

These graves are not the only markers of the occult in Athens. When interconnected on a map of the city, the five cemeteries form a path in the shape of a pentagram. The pentagram has long been associated with evil of all sorts, but the symbol has, since ancient times, been one of great religious significance. The Hebrews saw the five-pointed star as a symbol of truth, with its five points representing the books of the Pentateuch. The city of Jerusalem employed the symbol as its seal. Early Christians also adopted the sign, using its five points as a reminder of the five wounds of Christ. In ancient Greece, the followers of Pythagoras saw the pentagram as the pent-alpha, formed by five A's and incorporating the golden ratio. Medieval worshippers saw the pentagram as an "endless knot" that stood for truth and protection against demons. It was worn as an amulet, both for the person and the home. Even witches, who are often associated with evil intentions, view the pentagram as a symbol of noble empowerment, able to provide both knowledge and protection. Its five points represent the elements: spirit, water, fire, earth and air.

The pentagram formed by the cemeteries in Athens has been said to create a safety zone against evil, protecting the city and its people from forces that might threaten their safety. The zone supports the views of the spiritualists who believed that Athens was a highly spiritual place, an area where courageous, able and strong individuals were able to contact the mystics and have the past, present and future revealed to them. As a result, some believe that when chaos strikes in the form of earthquakes, fires and floods that destroy the monuments of man, Athens will remain untouched. The spirit world, however, can intervene in the lives of those who stumble upon misfortune.

Take, for example, the story of an OU student. For nights on end, he experienced the same dream involving a lady in white who warned against accepting a friend's offer of a ride on a motorcycle. Days later, he suddenly realized why he'd been visited by this persisting vision. A friend of his did in fact ride up to his home one day to ask if he would like to accompany him on a motorcycle ride through the country. Remembering the lady in white, the student refused. A short time later, his friend crashed into a tree and died. The student's life had been saved by his recurring dream.

Fox Family Channel named Athens as one of the United States' scariest places in 2000. Needless to say, some of the many accounts are legends that have been exaggerated over time, as myths tend to be. Details are changed, gore is amplified, tragedy is multiplied. But regardless of how the stories have evolved over time, the obscuring of the facts does not diminish the firm belief in the powerful presence of the paranormal in Athens.

Smyrna Cemetery

Years ago, before settlers began to populate Clermont County, Native American tribes such as the Shawnee held free reign over the land. Richard Crawford describes how the area drew tribes because of its proximity to the Ohio River and its bountiful forests. Permanent settlements were out of the question; the climate was simply too humid and the land too swampy. Even if they had wanted to establish something more a seasonal village, tribes would have had to compete for land with the steady stream of European settlers expanding westward from the northern Atlantic coast. As settlement increased, conflict was inevitable between the newcomers and the land's original inhabitants.

The Shawnee attempted to keep the Ohio River as a permanent border between themselves and the foreigners. They soon realized that it was more prudent to move further north into what would eventually become the state of Ohio. Under the direction of their leader and shaman, Sweet Lips, the tribe established a village on the site of what is now the Smyrna Cemetery. From there, they continued to harass and to attack the incoming white settlers.

One Christmas Eve 1787, Sweet Lips ordered an assault that would prove the beginning of her downfall. A surveying party was attacked by Sweet Lips' tribe at their campsite, which, according to Richard Crawford, was on the present-day site of the Felicity–Franklin High School. There, a fierce skirmish ensued when the Shawnee pounced upon the unsuspecting enemy. Casualties were many, but Crawford notes that there were no reported deaths.

The tribe managed to take Peter Hastings, one of the surveyors, prisoner. The hapless man was brought to the village where his body was painted black in preparation for his execution. What happened next is still the source of some mystery; Sweet Lips, for unknown reasons, spared Hastings' life. She wasn't quite willing to condemn the man to death. Was it compassion? Was it kindness? Regardless, as time passed it became clear to all that Hastings had impressed Sweet Lips. He even convinced her to release him and allow him to escape. He claimed that he would return, and Sweet Lips, eager to provide an incentive, promised Hastings land if he did. Why Sweet Lips would allow Hastings to escape on the condition that he return is an interesting question for which there is no answer. Did Hastings find a way into Sweet Lips' affections, winning her heart to win his freedom?

Hastings did return, albeit seven years later, in 1795, shortly after the Treaty of Greeneville, which forced the Native Americans to surrender the southern two-thirds of the present state of Ohio. Hastings made a triumphant return, visiting the Shawnee not as a prisoner of war, but as a victor. He stopped in to see Sweet Lips to make sure she followed through on her promise of land.

The promise came as a revelation to the Shawnee, who were never informed of the arrangement. Already incensed at having to leave their home, the tribe was further infuriated by their belief that their leader had, in effect, betrayed them. They turned on Sweet Lips, deciding to execute her before moving north of the Greeneville Treaty Line.

Although accounts vary as to how Sweet Lips met her death, no scenario would have been agreeable for the fallen shaman. One account claimed that she was forced to dig her own grave. When finished, she kneeled at its edge and was then bludgeoned with a tomahawk blow to her neck. Her body then fell into the grave. Another claimed that she met

The spirit of a betrayed Shawnee Indian woman wanders around Smyrna Cemetery in Clermont County.

the same fate as had originally been planned for the prisoner Peter Hastings. Her body was painted black and then she was tied to a stake and burnt. Her charred remains were buried. Her tribe continued on its way north, only to watch their way of life fade under the influence of the white settlers. But while the Shawnee and others were herded onto reservations far from their ancestral homes, one among them has chosen to remain in Smyrna.

Even now, Sweet Lips continues to make her presence felt. On foggy, moonlit nights, people passing near Smyrna Cemetery have claimed that a woman in Indian dress can be

seen wandering around the tombstones, searching for something. For what? No one knows. Some speculate she is looking
for the tribe that abandoned her so many years ago. Perhaps
she seeks forgiveness for her promise to Hastings. Whatever
the reason, it seems that Sweet Lips' fate is to wander the land
of her former home.

The Horseshoe Tombstone

In Otterbein Cemetery, half a mile south of Route 22 in Perry
County, there is a tombstone inscribed with the name of
Mary Henry, who died on February 28, 1845. On the back of
this particular tombstone, there is a mysterious rusty red
stain in the shape of a horseshoe. What's odd is that this
tombstone is Mary Henry's second and that the same red
horseshoe mark appeared on her first one. What does it all
mean? The horseshoe, which at times has been described as
bloody, is a symbol of death—of a jealousy played out to its
most extreme.

The story begins in 1844 when young James Henry began
feeling that he wanted to marry. Unfortunately, he had a little
problem. He was in love with two women and could not bring
himself to choose between the two. Finally, after weeks of
deliberation, he made up his mind. Or rather, his horse did.

Henry loved horses and was very close to his animal. It
never strayed far from home, and if its master fell asleep in
the wagon, the horse would lead him home. One night,
however, the horse took Henry not to his home, but to the
home of one his girls. He took it as a sign—fate illuminating
the path he was meant to take. His mind was made up; he
would ask for the girl's hand in marriage. It helped too that

A horse plays a prominent role in the tragic story of James and Mary Henry.

she was fanatical about horses, spending almost any time she had to herself mounted atop her horse. The two were married.

Were they happy? Were they able to enjoy the fruits of wedded bliss? These are questions without answers. Regardless, their union was short-lived. Life expectancy wasn't quite what is today, and Henry's wife became ill and succumbed to death shortly thereafter. Her passing deeply affected Henry, leading him to spend countless hours sitting next to her grave in Otterbein Cemetery, flowers in hand, disconsolate and inconsolable. If he wasn't in the cemetery, he was riding her horse, the living embodiment of their life and love together. Friends and family wondered whether James would ever be happy again. They did everything they could to reach him, but his misery persisted, bearing down upon him with all the weight of the world.

While mourning one day at Mary's grave, Henry encountered a figure from his recent past, one who understandably had the ability to mend a broken heart. The figure was none other than the woman Henry had passed over when he chose Mary to be his bride. She had clung to the hope that someday they might be together again. Mary's death, while tragic, had allowed the embers of her love for Henry to flame again. Certainly she couldn't expect him to forget to Mary so quickly and so easily, but who knew what could happen with time?

In time, Henry not only learned to laugh again but fell madly in love. The friendship turned passionate, and marriage soon followed. Yet, as happy as Henry was, his memories of Mary were never far from his mind. No matter how much his bride asked, begged or demanded that he make a clean break and get rid of Mary's horse, he refused. Mary's love and spirit would continue to be honored. Of course, even if Henry had been willing to let go of the past, it didn't seem as if the past was willing to let go of him.

A friend walking by Otterbein Cemetery one evening glanced quickly at Mary's tombstone and stopped to get a closer look. He rubbed his eyes, squinted and gawked. But there was no mistaking what he saw. There, on the tombstone, was the mark of a bloody horseshoe. Fear spread through his soul, inflaming a desire to warn Henry. He made his way to Henry's home and recounted what he had seen, concluding that he believed the mark to be an omen, a portent of grave misfortune. Henry dismissed the warning as nothing but speculation and conjecture fueled by paranoia. His friend could do nothing to convince Henry of what he believed so deeply to be true. He left, his heart still filled with a dreadful unease.

That night, under the shadow of clouds that had been gathering all day long, the weather turned frightful. The townspeople were assailed by violent winds, whipping rain and awesome thunder and lightning. By morning, the skies had cleared and the Henrys decided that they would go into town.

Directing his wife to wait, Henry went out to the barn to hitch Mary's horse to his buggy. He would return momentarily to enjoy a hearty warm breakfast. His wife sat down to wait for Henry to return. But he didn't return. The eggs, cooked sunny side up, hardened. Bacon fat congealed in the cast iron skillet. Mugs of coffee turned cold. His wife, her patience at an end, went out to the barn to investigate her husband's tardiness. Upon entering the barn, she knew that something was wrong. The interior was far too quiet.

Mr. Henry lay face down in the hay behind his first wife's horse. Puzzled, Mrs. Henry yelled at him to get up since they were due in town. There was no response. She nudged him gently and, finally, rolled him over onto his back. The screams were enough to bring her neighbors running. Mr. Henry was dead, his face revealing the reason why. His first wife's horse had kicked him, its horseshoe print revealing quite plainly where it had done so.

Mr. Henry was buried in Otterbein Cemetery, his soul ready to rejoin Mary in the afterlife. It seemed that Mary couldn't stand the thought of her husband being with her long-time rival. Or maybe it was a horrible accident. Regardless, the stain on the tombstone continues to appear, even though the stone has been replaced again and again. And it's believed that on foggy nights, out on Otterbein Road, the sound of hoofbeats on the pavement can be heard up and down the street. Apparently, Mary and James are riding her horse again, much as they did together in life.

5

Haunted by History

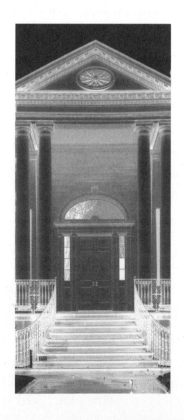

~

We are the product as well as the producers of history. The present is constantly receding into the past, and we continue to look to our pasts to inform our futures. Ghosts are artifacts—relics from the past that we find both foreign and familiar. Apparitions from years long past offer us a glimpse into a world that, for most of us, exists only in textbooks and the imagination. Historical ghost stories allow us to journey back in time and experience the extraordinary. In the following accounts, history provides the backdrop for a surprising variety of individual struggles— all of which do justice to Ohio's rich heritage.

~

The Runaway Slave

During the Civil War, while Union and Confederate troops fought for supremacy in bloody clashes such as Gettysburg and Shiloh, a war of another sort was being fought by civilians. The issue: slavery. Contrary to popular belief, views on slavery in the Union states were far from uniform. In fact, Southern sympathizers across the North proved themselves a formidable presence, creating secret societies and clans whose allegiances lay elsewhere.

Ohio, a Union state, suffered internal strife as politicians such as Clement L. Vallandigham decalred that the war was being fought not to preserve the Union, but to confer freedom upon the Negro and enslave the whites. Vallandigham was not alone; in Ohio's gubernatorial elections of 1863, he drew wide support when he ran as a candidate for the Peace Democrats. Other pro-slavery advocates, such as the Knights of the Golden Circle and the Copperheads, also waged ideological warfare.

Athens was not immune to this sort of subversion. Split as it was over the issue of slavery, those harboring fugitive slaves necessarily became targets for the wrath of those fighting to preserve the institution. Southern sympathizers could focus their actions on several local houses that served as stops along the Underground Railroad. Here was the Civil War writ small.

At some point prior to or during the Civil War, a house on 24 East Washington Street was raided. Southern sympathizers had realized that the house—still the oldest in Athens—was indeed a stop along the Underground Railroad. A mob assembled and attacked the home with guns brandished. Alarmed by the sound of thundering footsteps and strident voices, a slave named Nicodemus listened from behind a false wall in a hidden tunnel. He peered with one eye through the slats, trying to discern the mob's movements by their flickering torches. His heart pounded, its beat echoing through his skull like a death knell. The seconds passed slowly, turning imperceptibly into minutes, first one, then two and before long ten. Before long, the house fell silent. The voices became distant and the footsteps faded into nothingness. Nicodemus couldn't be sure the house was empty, but he knew that he had to make his way to the basement tunnels and escape to safety.

His hands trembled and his feet quaked, but he finally managed to ease open the false wall, pausing every second to reassure himself that he was alone. He crept out from behind the wall and began making his way towards the basement. Unfortunately, Nicodemus realized a little too late that he wasn't alone. From the corner of his eye, he saw a man and then heard voices raised in alarm. The floor shook again with the thunder of footsteps, and he heard the unmistakable sound of gun hammers clicking into place. Nicodemus' mind was filled with only one thought: run. And he did. But as he ran, he became an easy target. After he heard the gunshot, pain flared through his leg and chest. Nicodemus collapsed in a heap on the floor and died only moments later as the mob dragged his body through the house.

It's not clear what happened immediately following Nicodemus' death. What we do know is that the home survived and that over a century later, in 1972, Nicodemus returned, offering a sorority a lesson no one could have anticipated.

In the fall of 1972, 24 East Washington Street was home to an Ohio University sorority, Zeta Tau Alpha. As Halloween approached, the members wanted to do something a little different than throw a costume party or set out bowls of produce disguised as internal organs. Instead, they invited a local witch to divine their futures from tarot cards. The witch arrived on the appointed day, and upon crossing the threshold of the home, she exclaimed that she felt the presence of long dead man still within. She may have awakened the long dormant spirit, for it wasn't long before the tenants of the house began experiencing unusual things.

One girl was sleeping one afternoon when she was awakened by the odd but very real sensation that hands around her neck were attempting to squeeze the life out of her. Although the room was empty, the girl remained convinced that someone was trying to kill her. She ran from her room and the sensation mysteriously stopped. Later that year, another resident claimed that she had seen the figure of a man, about six feet four inches tall, tramping about the house. Of course, men did occasionally visit the sorority house, but the girl was struck by how ragged and torn this man's clothing was. A group was mobilized to search the house for this apparent intruder. But after poring over every corner of every room, nothing was found. The man had vanished.

The ghostly visitations continued well past the Christmas break. They were soon accompanied by sounds—sometimes a quiet whine, other times scratching from behind walls and sealed-off passage entrances. Then objects began disappearing from bedrooms. After theft was ruled out, the disappearances could only be attributed to the mysterious apparition. Eventually, doors began to swing open on their own; once again, a search of the sorority turned up nothing but a house full of terrified—and slightly annoyed—sisters. While the events in the house were still somewhat troubling, their frequency was breeding familiarity.

The girls decided that they had to accept the runaway slave. It wasn't long before they embraced Nicodemus and began leaving notes for him and whispering goodnight to him as they drifted off to sleep.

When the Zeta Tau Alpha chapter closed in 1988, it was replaced by the Sigma Nu fraternity and, later, the Alpha Omicron Pi sorority. Today, 24 East Washington Street is home to the Sigma Phi Epsilon fraternity, and Nicodemus seems to have faded into memory. The AOPs maintain that they never experienced anything out of the ordinary. But who knows? Perhaps after the Sigma Phis settle into their new fraternity house, Nicodemus may once again roam the house in which he was killed.

Zoar Village

The small community of Zoar was founded in 1817 by a group of 200 German Separatists seeking religious freedom from their homeland. In Germany, the group's religious beliefs had led to persecution—a situation aggravated by the publication of *The Separatist Principles*. The settlers landed at Philadelphia in August 1817, led by Joseph Bimeler. Upon arrival, Bimeler purchased, at three dollars an acre, 5,000 acres of land in the Tuscarawas Valley in Ohio. The first of his congregation arrived on October 16, 1817. They christened their new home Zoar, the town to which Lot had fled when Sodom was destroyed by fire and brimstone. As their symbol, the group used the seven-pointed star of Bethlehem and the acorn, from which grows the mighty oak tree. Few could have predicted that ghosts from the community would one day make Zoar popular with tourists.

Initially, the Separatists relished the freedom to practice their beliefs in America. But creating a home in the wilderness was far from simple; the community's imminent failure loomed over Zoar like the sword of Damocles, casting a pall on all that Bimeler and his followers had worked so hard to achieve. But the people were not quite ready for the sun to set on their great experiment. In 1819, they devised a plan to make all property and earnings common. This plan established the Society of Separatists of Zoar. When Bimeler was named Agent-General, his position as the spiritual and temporal leader was further entrenched. The community was bolstered by many liberal beliefs. Both men and women, for example, were allowed a vote and the chance to hold office. With this newfound direction, Zoar weathered its troubles and even began to thrive.

By the middle of the 19th century, Zoar was practically self-sufficient, possessed of assets totaling over one million dollars. But while the community was flourishing financially, the seeds of Zoar's downfall lay within its very success. Increased exposure to outsiders and their customs left a definite impression on the younger members of Zoar; it wasn't long before their altered values began to clash with the conservative traditions. Moreover, Zoar's businesses were unable to adapt to changing demands and times, losing key markets that they should have been able to maintain. The end came in 1898 when members voted to dissolve the society. Land and property was divided among former members and an auction was held to sell surplus livestock and farm equipment. The families had to return to eking out an existence for themselves. Zoar itself became simply another small town dedicated to life, liberty and the pursuit of happiness in the American heartland.

Today, Zoar still exists. It is a community of about 75 families living in homes surviving from Zoar's early days as a religious haven. While the homes provide a visual complement to Zoar's past, it is the oral history and folklore that illuminates both the mind and the imagination, drawing out threads of the past lingering within the collective unconscious. Here in Zoar, figures from the past continue to move about the village as if mortality and time had never reached out with their stony grips and pushed them headlong into death. The historic buildings are still inhabited by those who lived so many, many years ago. Jenny Pavlasek, writing in the October 2000 issue of *Ohio Magazine,* recounts some of the stories in and around Zoar Village.

Take, for example, the Zoar Hotel. In its day, the establishment was the place to be. A non-Separatist by the name of

The historic Zoar Hotel

Alexander Gunn held large and rambunctious parties, fetes that would last well into the early hours of the morning and sometimes beyond. He lived at the hotel in the late 1800s, and despite his differing religious beliefs and nationality, was accepted by the society. Guests at Gunn's celebrations included the likes of William McKinley and his alleged mistress. But while the hotel has long since been abandoned, there are three permanent guests who still reside within its halls. One is allegedly Alexander Gunn. Even in death, the party continues for the great socialite, who returns every so often to see how everything is proceeding. McKinley's supposed mistress is another spirit who returns, and she is sometimes joined by a woman who was fondly known in life as Mother Rouf, but properly recognized as Mary Rouf. She first came to the hotel as a young child and took charge of the hotel after the society disbanded. Rouf assumed possession when communal property was dispersed among the former members. She ran the hotel until her death in 1919, and, strangely enough, the hotel became less and less successful with each passing year after her death. Eventually it closed down.

But even though the Zoar Hotel is no longer open, visitors looking for a place to stay might be advised to try the Cowger House, a bed and breakfast in the second log cabin built by the Separatists. Built for the brewmaster, the building is the oldest existing building in Zoar. Owned by Mary and Ed Cowger, the inn has been in operation for about 16 years, and one guest in particular is unwilling to leave the place just yet. While painting a bedroom in the place late one evening, Mary heard the front door open and footsteps make their way up the stairs. Whoever was climbing the stairs greeted Mary, proclaiming loudly, "Honey, I'm back." Thinking it was her husband, Mary called out but never got a response in return. When she called home, she was surprised to discover that her husband hadn't even been to the bed and breakfast all night; he was in bed at home and had been for quite some time. Ed came back to the inn to see for himself exactly what was going on, but could find nothing. Everything in the inn had been left how he had left it. Whoever had spoken with Mary obviously had no need for walls or barriers. He could just pass right through them. Since that time, guests and the Cowgers have

The Zoar Hotel is haunted by three ghosts, including that of Alexander Gunn, once a prominent socialite.

both encountered PJ, an old, gentlemanly ghost who can be best identified by his purple jacket. When a guest heard the stories about PJ from the Cowgers, the startled man was certain they had just described his father, who had once owned the building. PJ, it seems, has not yet left the building.

At Books 'n' Things, a second-hand bookstore in the former home of the village tinsmith, shoppers might have a firsthand encounter with the spirit world. Three sisters moved to Zoar close to 16 years ago and opened up the bookstore and its accompanying tea room. From the start, each sister began experiencing unusual things that they kept secret from one another. None wanted to be considered crazy by the others. But once they opened themselves up to each other, they realized that their experiences weren't quite so unusual after all. One sister was upstairs one night when she caught the scent of coffee wafting up from down below. Always up for a cup of coffee, the sister padded down the stairs to the kitchen. But once there, she found that the kitchen was in complete darkness; more surprisingly, there was no sign of anyone having made a pot of coffee. The pot sat where the sisters had last left it, and it was cold to the touch. If there was no freshly brewed coffee for the sister to smell, then what, exactly, did she smell that night? Another of the sisters was in bed one evening when she distinctly felt someone sit down at the foot of her bed, though she couldn't see anyone there. But the mattress had definitely moved, since the sheets had indents to indicate that someone had sat down. Shortly after, rockers began rocking on their own and children's books had their pages turned without any assistance from a reader.

At the Inn on the River, the unexplained takes the shape of flying plates and glasses. It seems that the resident spirit, George, does not like to be taken lightly. One evening, an actor was hired to portray the inn's spirit, allegedly a man who drowned to death when he fell off a canal boat near Zoar. When the actor walked into the room, a picture inexplicably flew by his head. Apparently, George found the man's impersonation of him insulting. At other times, customers have watched in panic as bottles fly from the bar. But George can

Although Zoar was unable to preserve its founding principles, the spirits of the past have never left the community.

have his lighter moments too. The songs of Patsy Cline are sometimes heard wafting gently from the jukebox speakers. She must be one George's favorites, because there are no Patsy Cline records or discs in the jukebox.

Contemporary Zoar is a far cry from what Joseph Bimeler had envisioned when he first arrived in the Tuscarawas Valley early in the 19th century. Although his great experiment failed, it lives on in the buildings and architecture of today's Zoar. But something else lives on too, some paranormal energy—as charged and alive as anything living.

Sorg Opera House

It is the nature of things to change, sometimes for the better, sometimes for the worse. When it's the latter, we cleave to the past more tightly, looking back to a time when life was simple and uncomplicated. We seek the sights, sounds and scents of our memories, longing for a time when cultures were distinct and unique, when the homogenization of the American town had not yet begun. In Middletown, the struggle between tradition and progress plays itself out in a vintage opera house, where a former pillar of the community still haunts one of the town's most interesting buildings.

Daniel Doty, the father of Middletown, first settled in the area when he arrived from New Jersey with his family in 1796; but it was Stephen Vail who, in 1802, set aside 52 of 100 acres for development. He named the land Middle-town, anticipating that the town along the Great Miami River would eventually be roughly equidistant from both Dayton and Cincinnati. People began arriving upon the completion of the Miami–Erie Canal. The waterway was a vast improvement over rutted roads and the Great Miami River, and also connected the tiny community with Dayton and Cincinnati. Begun in 1825, the canal extended from Lake Erie to the Ohio by 1845. Middletown thrived until the arrival of the railroad lines—the steel arteries that proved to be better lifelines than the canals. The last canal boat left Middletown in 1906.

While other communities lived and died with the canals, Middletown continued to prosper. In 1900, George M. Verity founded the American Rolling Mill Company on Doty's Grove, and began churning out the first of what would amount to 135 million tons of steel. As people flocked to

Middletown in search of work, its population exploded from 9215 in 1900 to 29,992 in 1930. Middletown owed its existence to these factories; Verity funded the construction of public buildings, schools, parks, public works and a community center, following an example set by Middletown's first millionaire and the second wealthiest man in Ohio, Paul John Sorg, sometimes known as "the Last of the Robber Barons."

At one time, Sorg was Middletown's largest employer, with generations of Middletonians laboring in his tobacco plant, paper mill and hotel. His 35-room mansion, constructed in 1888, is still considered a fine example of Romanesque architecture, and remains the centerpiece of a block of Victorian homes. Sorg's money helped future governor James Cox to establish the cornerstone of a media empire when he lent his former employee $6000 to purchase the *Dayton Daily News*, the first acquisition in what would become Cox Enterprises. Sorg died on May 28, 1902, and was interred at Woodside Cemetery in the city he had helped, at the very least, to sustain.

The Middletown he left behind is a far cry from the Middletown that is struggling to right itself today. After years of dependence upon the steel and paper industries, Middletown's businesses are no longer thriving. The times are changing, never more poignantly illustrated than when Sorg Paper closed in May 2000 after 148 years in business. In 1961, the American Rolling Mill Company, which had become Armco, employed more than 50,000 people in 139 countries, 8000 of them in Middletown. Today, Armco is AK Steel. While it is still the largest employer in Middletown with 4100 workers, workers constantly face the threat of a shutdown. No longer do the people of Middletown look upon the company as the lifeline of its city. Its role as a paternal benefactor has slowly eroded over the years as concerns about community have given way to those fiscal. In 2000, the Environmental Protection Agency filed suit against AK Steel, accusing it of air, water and solid-waste pollution. Eventually the case was dismissed, but the fact that Middletonians were joining the fight against AK Steel revealed how much the relationship between industry and community had changed.

A walk on the main downtown thoroughfare of Central Avenue reveals a promenade of empty storefronts and abandoned buildings, a far cry from the strip where Middletonians from all walks and stations of life used to congregate for food, entertainment and company. Its main shopping attraction, the City Center Mall, was built in 1973 but never managed to capture the hearts of Middletonians; its forbidding interior was about as attractive as a dark alleyway. Instead, people were drawn to the freeway artery east of downtown, where a number of businesses have relocated from the city center. Middletown followed suit, buying land along the Interstate 75 and the Ohio 122. Following extensive commercial development, the population grew and money began to roll in.

But downtown boosters have not abandoned hope. City Center Mall is having its mall structure removed to make way for a four-block renovation of the downtown sector. Its estimated cost is $13 million. Others are hoping that businesses such as professional offices will be attracted by vacant office space and that young professionals will be drawn downtown by the conversion of some empty buildings into loft apartments. The hope is that these new tenants will restore some of Middletown's former glory. Maybe city planners should take a look at South Main Street where the past never left, where it is still possible to step back in time and remember a time when Middletonians had something to call their own. It was a time when Paul John Sorg was the Middletown millionaire, and when the city's downtown district attracted individuals from all walks of life by the thousands. Some came to shop or to eat; others came to be entertained in the Sorg Opera House.

Jennie Sorg, Paul's wife, was allegedly a lover of the arts, high and low. She wanted a venue that would lure performers from New York to perform in Middletown. So, in 1891, Paul Sorg unveiled a working opera house, presented as a gift to his wife and to the citizens of Middletown. It would be used as a concert hall, but would also be available for all worthwhile causes. People came from all over Ohio and the Midwest to see names such as Will Rogers, Marie Dressler, Bob Hope and John Philip Sousa perform. And like any other sophisticated venue, rules and etiquette needed to be observed while in the Sorg Opera House.

In *Haunted Ohio,* Chris Woodyard points out that blacks had to enter the theater through a separate entrance and were only allowed in the second balcony. Women, on the other hand, were not allowed on the second balcony to protect them from the unruly characters they might find there. It's said that when restoration work was being done there, workers had to shovel the tobacco juice out of the area. Patrons sitting throughout the rest of the building were required to wear full evening dress.

From 1915 to 1986, the house showed movies in addition to stage and opera acts. It began to show movies full-time in 1929. It is now home to the Sorg Opera Company, and Middletown is the second smallest city in American with a professional company. The building is a reminder of its heyday; restoration work has ensured that Paul Sorg's vision remains accessible even now, more than a century later. It has survived two brushes with fire, and even though he has been dead for a century now, Paul John Sorg continues to frequent the opera house bearing his name.

To encounter his spirit is to remember Middletown's past. Resplendent in his evening finery, the patron of Middletown invariably sits in the center seat of his first row. He has been spotted at various times over the years at both performances and rehearsals. In spite of the decline, Sorg has not yet abandoned Middletown.

No one knows what will happen with Middletown, whether or not it will continue to be two cities in one—one with a dormant downtown, the other with a hustling and bustling interstate artery. Sorg must be hoping that as people come to explore the subdivisions growing at the city's eastern edge, they too will discover the little things about the community that are just waiting to astound them in the downtown core. Until that time, he will continue to occupy the best seat in the Sorg Opera House.

Loveland Castle

As the years roll on, the past acquires a rosy glow. Nostalgia renders our memories immune to the anxieties and concerns that plague us, and we look at the past longingly. The Romantics longed for the innocence of youth; the Classicists yearned for the grandeur of ancient Greece. Of course, the past is past. Or is it?

Harry Andrews wanted to bring the past to life by re-creating a time when chivalry wasn't just a punchline, when honor comprised strength of both character and heart. From an early age, the Hamilton County building engineer had cultivated a love of all things medieval; he studied the period's architecture at Colgate University, and he found a refuge from the horrors of World War I in various European castles that served as medical headquarters. Immersed in the beauty of the medieval on one hand, and the awesome destruction of the war on the other, Andrews had an epiphany. He became convinced that his vision might help to save civilization. By the time Andrews returned to the United States, he bore the title of Sir, having been knighted by a French earl whose son he saved in France.

To complete his vision, Andrews drew upon his experience as Boy Scout troop leader, when he led a group of youngsters named the Knights of the Golden Trail. One of his favorite activities was camping, and Andrews often brought his young charges to the banks of the Little Miami River for that purpose. Some of his scouts' parents recognized how important this time was to Andrews, and when the *Cincinnati Enquirer* offered to exchange a plot of land along the riverbank for a year's paid subscription, a number of families took advantage. In turn, they donated

Medieval enthusiast Harry Andrews spent more than half a century building Loveland Castle.

the lots to Andrews and the Boy Scouts. Andrews' troop quickly became a semi-permanent fixture along the Little Miami, so much so that it soon seemed pointless to keep packing and unpacking their equipment again and again. Andrews constructed two stone tents to house the equipment and provide shelter during inclement weather. Years later, his idea to protect the camping gear would inspire something much grander.

Andrews would construct a castle, the architectural embodiment of his chivalric vision. And he would create a group of men dedicated to promoting a medieval code of life, based on the Ten Commandments, which would become one of the pillars of his new civilization. He would name them the Knights of the Golden Trail, and their vision would become a reality on the banks of the Little Miami River.

Using the layout of a castle he had seen in France, Chateau LaRoche, Andrews set about creating an exact replica of the structure from the ground up. Eschewing ready-made bricks, he waded into the Little Miami River to haul out nearly 50,000 buckets of stones from its depths. These were mixed with cement, and the combination was left to dry and set inside discarded milk cartons. Starting in 1929, Andrews used his bricks to build his castle; the work occupied more than half a century. While some believe he placed every brick himself, Andrews did have some assistance. With the help of his knights, Andrews was able to construct a 17-room castle, complete with a great hall, a banquet hall, an armory, a master bedroom, a chapel, gardens and even its own dungeon. It had four main rooms and measured 96 feet by 65 feet. Andrews died in 1981 before he was able to complete his castle.

Like knights rallying around their fallen king, the Knights of the Golden Trail took it upon themselves to realize their founder's dream. Andrews' ideal became their mission. To this day, the members continue to build a roof to span the north wing and extending walls. Nine years after Andrews' death, the castle was opened to the public, with admission fees used to support the completion of the last floor of one wing's tower and the general maintenance of what is now a historic landmark. Inside, the castle looks much the same as it did when Andrews shed his mortal coil. Modern amenities are nowhere in evidence, since the use of modern appliances was a betrayal of Andrews' vision—an inexcusable offence when you consider that Andrews hasn't yet left the building.

His death has inspired a number of myths and legends. One claims that Andrews was an immigrant from Europe who moved to the States. The castle was a replica of one he had often visited with his girlfriend before he emigrated. It was his hope that the castle would entice his love to come to him in America, and with 17 rooms of the castle completed, he sent for her. She refused to join him, and Andrews, unable to do anything else, dedicated himself to work on the castle. He died working on it and his spirit continues to haunt his monument to unrequited love. Others believe that he caught fire while burning leaves in his garden and was killed, forever trapping his ghost within the building.

Was his death so spectacularly tragic? Probably not. Regardless of how he died, Andrews is rumored to haunt his castle. People have reported cold spots in the dungeon and have claimed that being in the castle can be an eerie experience. It seems that even in death, Andrews is unable to give up his obsessions. Perhaps he takes comfort in the sight of his knights continuing his life's work with the same simplicity and care.

Utopia

Utopia, a Clermont County village that borders Brown County, was founded in 1844 when Judge Wade Loofborough purchased 1140 acres of land saddling the Ohio River. He and others had come to seek a new civilization protected from the evils of mechanization and industrialization. Loofborough and his followers, after all, were ardent supporters of the ideas and philosophy of the Frenchman Charles Fourier.

Condemning existing institutions, Fourier sought to realize a sort of utopian socialism, wherein the natural instincts and passions of humanity would be directed, channeled and guided toward social harmony. It would be a society based on agriculture, in which individuals would both live and work together, where work would be divided among people according to their natural inclinations. Loofborough sought a utopia where none would want for anything and everyone helped one another.

In keeping with Fourier's recommendations, Loofborough and his group built themselves a two-story brick building with 30 rooms or, as Fourier might have said, a phalanstery. With the home complete and the members willing, the great experiment began. Two years later, it was over.

By 1846, Loofborough realized that success was highly unlikely. Seeking some way to salvage the cost of their failure, the group sold the land to John O. Wattles, a leader of a community of 100 spiritualists. As the Fourierites had before them, the spiritualists sought a place in which they could construct their own vision of a perfect society.

The spiritualists believed that no one man or woman really dies. While corporeal beings may decay, their spirits survive, existing somewhere in the ether, as alive as ever. In order to communicate with the spirits, their words had to be filtered through a medium. The souls of the dead could speak with the living through written messages, manifestations, trance-speaking, spirit-photography and music. The afterlife was not a simple demarcation between heaven and hell; instead, it was a series of progressions for the soul.

Wattles was a medium, blessed with the ability to speak with the spirits. But while he could converse with the alleged dead, Wattles' skills at engineering were questionable at best.

When the spiritualists took possession of the brick house, they decided to move it closer to the river and to add a story and a basement. Reconstruction was finished quickly and the night of December 13, 1847, was set for the compound's housewarming. The place was filled with spiritualists, all gathered to celebrate the beginning of something new and grand. It wasn't long, however, before someone began to notice that water was beginning to trickle in slowly, but steadily, across the floor. And then, without warning, water from the Ohio poured in through whatever crack or fissure it could fill, overrunning the home and all within it.

The flash flood exacted its toll. It's been estimated that only six people survived the horrible catastrophe. There's no way to know for certain, of course, but it seems plausible, since the home still stands at what is now 3678 U.S. 52. More importantly, based on accounts dating back to the early 20th century, the place is apparently frequented by the spirits of six individuals, all dressed in soaking wet period garb. One lady, the most conspicuous, wears a blue dress and bonnet.

Richard Crawford, a historian and writer in Clermont County, writes about the similar experiences of generations of families who have lived in the Wattles house since 1917.

Founded upon the principles of utopian socialism, Utopia is better known for its paranormal lore today.

Wattles' room is believed to have been in the second floor bedroom. People in this room have reported to Crawford that they felt a pervasive sense of drowsiness there. They would enter a state that wasn't quite sleep and yet not quite consciousness. In this state, individuals have reported seeing a group of six people approaching along a dirt road, entering the house and walking up the staircase to the bedroom. As they approach the room, the group fades away. Invariably, witnesses see the woman in blue, sometimes accompanied by a man in Amish-type clothing and a young boy.

Crawford, who has spent a lot of time at the house, has written about the home and made it the subject of an annual Halloween show. Recently, he had the most peculiar time at the house as he and a film crew put on period clothing in preparation for a shoot.

"The owner's daughter," says Crawford, "who couldn't have been more than three or four, just started jumping up and down, saying she wanted to be on television." Her mother reprimanded the girl, telling her to stay out of the way and to leave the crew alone. Filming was delayed a number of times because of the girl's intrusions, but the mother insisted that her daughter not hear any of the stories surrounding their home. They might very well have terrified her. Finally, after two hours, Crawford and the crew completed their shooting in Wattles' room. Suddenly, the door opened and in burst the little girl.

The exasperated mother looked at the girl and asked what she wanted so badly. Crawford recalls that the girl asked her mother if she remembered what happened two nights earlier. The mother recalled that she had been baking and had asked her daughter to stop bothering her. The girl nodded and, according to Crawford's recollection, said, "Yes, and I didn't. I didn't even let the people who came to the door into the house. There were six people outside, and there was a lady in a blue dress with a blue bonnet. And they were all wet." Silence hung in the air. The girl, who hadn't been told any of the Wattles house stories, had just described the apparitions that people in the area had been seeing for years. "It was certainly unusual," says Crawford.

Something equally unusual happened recently when Crawford and a friend, Eddie Fox, visited the home. Upon arrival, Fox, who is a self-professed clairvoyant, walked oddly across the yard, constantly stopping and changing direction.

"When I got out of the car," says Fox, "I immediately sensed that there were nine to thirteen presences right there on the driveway, just waiting for us." Fox felt what he described as "very, very cold spots; I know there was something there." Crawford was puzzled by the behavior until Fox told him that he felt as if he were walking into people. But Fox could feel more than just the presence. He claimed that he could sense "how they think and how they feel." Asked to describe the spirits' collective mood, Fox answered, "I sensed anxiety and curiosity, and a feeling that they felt as if they were being invaded." Fox doesn't communicate directly with the beings he encounters, so he is unsure exactly why he feels the presence of three to seven more individuals than the six usually reported.

Perhaps he felt the psychic echo of a tragedy that had taken place over a century ago—the legacy of two failed attempts to establish a paradise on earth.

6
Public
Phantoms

~

Public places are shared spaces, so it's not surprising that a number of them count among their visitors spirits who remain tethered to the corporeal plane. Since these locales provided the settings in which entire lives were acted out, it's only natural that some of the characters have remained after death. And just as we will frequent a restaurant because we enjoy its food and atmosphere, ghosts seek out the familiar and the comfortable. Ghosts, after all, are not all that different from us. They are the souls and spirits of the once living, subject to the same desires as those who still draw breath. More than anything, their appearances in public places speak to their humanity.

~

The Moonville Ghost

Moonville no longer exists. It was once a railroad mining town, created when the Marietta and Cincinnati Route was built through the woods of southeastern Ohio in 1856. Soon it was discovered that the land was rich in natural resources, specifically coal and iron. Miners gravitated toward the area as industries sought to exploit the wealth of the land. By 1870, a community of 100 people, mostly miners and their families, had established the hamlet of Moonville.

The people made their homes along the railroad tracks, with a general store, saloon and sawmill just down Raccoon Creek. Those who weren't miners in Moonville worked in the Hope Furnace, where coal was used to aid in the manufacture of weapons and artillery for the Union Army during the Civil War. The town has long since rotted away; its structures are now artifacts of years past and a history that has faded from memory. But while the rotted timbers are now covered by nature's mantle, Moonville continues to exert a powerful hold on the imaginations of those living in Vinton County. The focus of their attention is a ghost of the past that continues to walk the land.

Andrew Henderson, a ghost hunter of sorts, came across an account from the *McArthur Democrat* dated March 31, 1859. An excerpt from the article reads:

A brakesman on the Marietta & Cincinnati railroad fell from the cars near Cincinnati Furnace, on last Tuesday, March 29, 1859, and was fatally injured, when the wheels passing over and grinding to a shapeless mass the greater part of one of his legs. He was taken on the train to Hamden and doctors…[were] sent for to perform amputation, but the prostration of the vital energies was too great to attempt it. The man is probably dead ere this. The accident resulted from a too free use of liquor.

It's at this point where history ends and speculation and conjecture begin. The drunken brakeman is believed to still walk the land, roaming the stretch of track where he was killed near the Moonville Tunnel. An article from the *Chillicothe Gazette* from 1895 records that

the ghost of Moonville, after an absence of one year, has returned and is again at its old pranks, haunting…freight trains and their crews. It appeared Monday night in front of fast freight No. 99…the ghost, attired in a pure white robe, carried a lantern. It had a flowing white beard, its eyes glistened like balls of fire and surrounding it was a halo of twinkling stars. When the train stopped, the ghost stepped off the track and disappeared into the rocks nearby.

Naturally, the ghost is said to be that of the brakeman. Or was he an engineer? A conductor or a signalman? Some have also wondered whether or not the man's death was an accident. The typical story begins with the brakeman drinking pint and after pint to go with games of poker in the local pub. Hours later, with a table of empty pint glasses to mark the passage of time, the brakeman staggered to his feet, his world awash in a beer-fueled haze. He stumbled out into the street and began making his way down the railroad tracks, his lantern's red glow dancing off the heavy rain. He felt the train's approach in the tunnel, and even in his inebriated state he was cognizant enough to recognize the danger to his life. But the train couldn't have been expected to stop in time, and it's not known if the engineer ever saw the brakeman frantically waving his lantern. In the lashing rain, visibility was extremely poor. The rest happened quickly. The brakeman lost his balance, fell on the tracks and his life, for all intents and purposes, was over. His body was buried in the Moonville graveyard, just west of town on top of a hill.

It wasn't long before people claimed that the brakeman's red lantern would cut through the darkness on rainy nights, shimmering near the Moonville Tunnel. But was the death an accident? There has been speculation that an engineer murdered the brakeman and had used the train to do so. In this story, the brakeman was asked to go under the train to inspect underneath. When he did, the engineer promptly started up the train and killed the man. Or perhaps the brakeman was actually trying to flag down the train to get it to drop off supplies for Moonville, which had been ravaged by the plague. His death, in this idealized and romanticized account, might very well have contributed to the decline of Moonville.

Regardless of the Moonville ghost's origins, a century later people still head to the train tracks in an attempt to find out exactly what it is that remains of Moonville.

Jeff Schmidt, who does not personally believe in ghosts and hauntings, did encounter something unusual during a trip to the Lake Hope state park. He had set off one weekend in 2000 to find the Moonville Tunnel and the cemetery. Happily, he discovered that the park offered a night hike to the Moonville Tunnel. He set off with his daughter to see for himself what exactly lurked out there. Once the group had reached the tunnel's center, they were told to turn off their flashlights; the darkness was complete. There, the story of the brakeman was recounted. Unfortunately, those who might have been hoping for a glimpse of his lantern were disappointed. Nothing unusual or unexplained took place in the tunnel. It wasn't until Schmidt visited the cemetery that something happened.

The day in question didn't seem unusual. The previous night's storms had cast a pall over the land. Schmidt snapped some photos while his daughter examined the gravestones. Only when his pictures were developed did he see something odd. Staring at one photo, he couldn't stop thinking about what he had heard about the brakeman. There in the photo was the image of something—an apparition, a specter—hovering above the ground. If it had been a sunny day, Schmidt would have simply "guessed it was the sun reflecting out of the camera's lens." But the day had been overcast and cloudy. Perhaps Schmidt had unwittingly captured the image of an orb, the visual indication of an unusual form of energy that can represent the presence of a spirit. Schmidt is still not convinced of the existence of spirits, but he does admit that he is unable to explain what appears in his photograph.

Andrew Henderson is also interested in finding the Moonville ghost. In July 1999, he and a friend drove down into the heavily forested Vinton County where "just turning off the highway was scary enough" for the pair. Following the path where the tracks of the Baltimore and Ohio route once lay, they set out into the night, armed with flashlights and a digital camera. Eventually, they came upon the tunnel; its entrance cut into a thickly forested ridge, a gaping maw in the midst of the wilderness. Henderson made an effort to speak to the ghost, but nothing happened. The two stayed at the tunnel for what felt like an hour, but heard or saw nothing scarier than geese in the river. While this initial trip was a failure, Henderson concedes that part of the legend claims that the night must be stormy before the brakeman will come out for a visit.

While both Henderson and Schmidt didn't find exactly what they'd been looking for, the woods of Moonville and the mysterious brakeman still exert a powerful grip upon their imaginations.

The Mysterious Yearling

The story of the Still House Hollow ghost is a peculiar one. Because it was first reported years ago, the line between fact and fiction may have been slightly blurred. Even so, it is still a compelling tale, and one with an unusual twist.

The city of Lancaster lies southeast of Columbus on the banks of the Hocking River. First incorporated in 1831, the town experienced its first real growth when the Lancaster Lateral Canal was opened to trade in 1836. Later, when markets opened to the east, an influx of wealth and opulence began. In 1854, the first two trains came into town from the C.W. & Z. Railroad and what is now the Indiana & Ohio. The bustling town was perfect for John Omsdorf, a wealthy Licking County stock dealer who relocated his trade in 1881. Unfortunately for Omsdorf, he wouldn't live to enjoy life in Lancaster for very long.

The facts become just a little hazy here. No one knows how or why, but one day Omsdorf's horse returned home without its rider. Omsdorf was missing, and the only thing to mark his absence was the disturbing sight of a horse covered with blood, brains and hair. It didn't require a great leap of faith to conclude that some horrible fate had befallen Omsdorf.

A trail of blood led from Foglesong Road to Still House Hollow at the city's northeastern edge. The trail went off the road, ultimately leading to a still house owned by a man named Crowley whose reputation was less than stellar. The farmers who had gathered outside the still were unable to push back the gnawing sense of dread eating away at their resolve. In the air, a smell hung so thick that some tried to brush it away from their nostrils. It didn't take the mob long to recognize the odor as that of sulfur—the emanations of hell itself, of fire and brimstone.

They pounded on the door and banged on the glass but there was no response. Crowley wasn't home. But the farmers were determined; their curiosity urged them on. In the end, they forced open the barred and locked house. Inside, they found no sign of Crowley or Omsdorf. But behind the house they found the carcass of a yearling calf. The mystery deepened, widening its net to encompass Omsdorf, Crowley and the dead cow. The two missing men were never heard from again. Or so it would seem. The cow, on the other hand, led a somewhat charmed afterlife.

One November night, as Pleasant Township resident Jacob Spangler rode his horse along Foglesong Road, he noticed something up ahead. As he approached, he thought the object in the road was a calf. On closer inspection, however, he couldn't decide what it was. The creature in front of him had the body of a calf, but there was something unusual about its head. The animal's eyes shimmered with more than just base intelligence; Spangler almost swore that they were human. And then there was the hair. The calf had a long, flowing mane of hair. Spangler claimed it was decidedly "unnatural." Spangler spurred his horse, but the animal refused to move. Then, oddly, the calf-creature mounted Spangler's steed, resting its front hooves on Spangler's shoulders. The horse rode off, and when it reached the southern edge of the road, the calf leapt off and disappeared into the darkness.

Shaken and disturbed, Spangler stopped in to see a Lancaster physician to make sure that he wasn't slowly losing his mind. Imagine his surprise, then, when the physician claimed that he'd seen the same strange creature. It wasn't long before other travelers on Foglesong Road began reporting the disturbing sight of the yearling calf with glowing eyes and unnaturally long hair. Only after the road was abandoned did the tale fade into obscurity. The mystery of the calf left more questions than answers. Was the strange calf the result of some sort of hellish ritual gone awry? Had the spirit, mind and perhaps body of either Crowley or Omsdorf fused onto the body of the yearling? Those searching for answers will probably have to content themselves with the mystery instead.

The Ashtabula Bridge Disaster

Chestnut Grove Cemetery contains four lots in which the remains of at least 25 people are interred in 19 coffins. A monument erected in 1896 honored the unrecognized dead 20 years after one of the worst train disasters in Ohio. The remains, still unidentified, are those of victims involved in what was called the Ashtabula Horror. But if reports from the Northeast Ohio Ghost Research Team are to be believed, the ghosts of those who perished in the crash feel that their sacrifice is worth more than a monument and burial in an anonymous plot.

It was four days after Christmas 1876, and the Lake Shore Pacific Express, a passenger train, was creeping towards the Ashtabula station along a Lake Shore & Michigan Southern line. The train was already two hours behind schedule, and station managers and expectant families were becoming impatient. Little did they know that the Lake Shore Pacific Express would never reach the Ashtabula station.

At around 7:30 PM, the train approached the Ashtabula River and the bridge bearing its name. A blizzard the day before had deposited mounds of snow along and across the tracks, and a wind blew fiercely through the air, whipping by at speeds of 40 miles an hour. Night had fallen, and darkness lay thick upon the land. As the lead engine began to cross the Ashtabula Bridge, the engineer felt something. He didn't want to believe what he'd sensed, but there was no denying what was happening beneath the train. The bridge was collapsing. The engineer stoked the fires of his engine, praying for time enough to bring the 11-car train to the other side safely. His engine gained the west side of the bridge, but when he looked back, he gaped in horror as the remaining passenger cars plummeted 60 feet into the river. The wooden cars, heated by coal stoves and illuminated with oil candles, erupted into flames upon impact, turning the passenger cars into funeral pyres. The engineer watched the fingers of flame as they curled around the wreckage; the flickering lights were accompanied by the cries and screams of trapped passengers.

The fire department was called in, but the deep snow had rendered some roads nearly impassable, impeding the rescuers' progress. By the time they managed to get their steam pump and engine down to the site, many had died. Like the engineer, the firemen stood watching the flames, consigning themselves to the fact that there was little they could do.

By morning, 92 of the 159 passengers had reached life's final destination. A special jury was convened that day to determine the cause of the terrible tragedy. After two months, the jury had come to a glaringly obvious, but at least official, conclusion. The accident and loss of life was the responsibility of Lake Shore & Michigan Southern Railway.

The problems began 11 years earlier when Charles Collins first looked over a bridge design proposal by Amasa Stone. Both men worked for Lake Shore & Michigan Southern as engineers. In Stone's design of the bridge, each truss, beam and means of support would work independently of the other—an experiment that differed greatly from typical bridges, where all the components are designed to support in unison. Although Collins recognized the design as experimental, he reluctantly approved Stone's proposal for the Howe Truss Bridge.

The decision would cost both men their lives. After Collins testified in court following the disaster, he was so overwhelmed by his mistake that he put a bullet in his head. Stone did the same a few years later. Perhaps the most

Victims of the Ashtabula train wreck are rumored to haunt the site of the calamitous tragedy.

distressing conclusion drawn by the jury was that the bridge was never carefully inspected by a competent bridge engineer. If it had been, then the structural defects would have been impossible to ignore. The railroad company's problems were compounded by the very real possibility that the casualties may not have been as numerous if the heating devices on the train had extinguished themselves upon collision, as the law required.

The collapse of Ashtabula Bridge was one of the worst tragedies of its kind in the 19th century. Even after the dead had been buried, some still suspected that not all those responsible had been brought to justice. They claimed that the fire had been allowed to burn so that the number of victims would remain a mystery. Many felt that the railroad company did not suffer enough for the pain and anguish it had so needlessly inflicted upon all concerned.

To its credit, the company dedicated four plots in the Chestnut Grove Cemetery for the dead and erected a monument to their honor on the 20th anniversary of the accident. They also halted construction of or replaced bridges that might be afflicted with the same sort of defects as the one that collapsed. But a decade had to pass before the company began to replace the dangerous coal and wood stoves in favor of steamers.

High above Chestnut Grove, the restless spirits of the Ashtabula Bridge disaster continue to search for reasons—for some sort of justification for their fates. Photographers snapping shots in the cemetery have captured the images of orbs and other unexplained phenomena, all suggesting that more than a century after the fact, the ghosts of Ashtabula have yet to find peace.

Enos Kay

Love is a funny thing. It can create and destroy bliss in moments, leaving bitterness where once there was none. In special cases, the wounds remain as fresh as the day they were opened, even long after the corporeal form has rotted away.

Enos Kay died in the late 19th century, but the sting of his lover's rejection has sustained his spirit through the years. He continues to roam Ross County, robbing lovers of the happiness denied him in life. When someone said that misery loves company, they might well have been thinking of Enos Kay.

The year was 1869. The setting was Egypt Pike, on the county line between Ross and Pickaway. Little distinguished Enos. He worked hard, went to church and, like most everyone else of his day, he wanted to find a woman he could love and protect and who would become the mother of his children. What set Enos apart from all the other eligible young men in town was that he had won the heart of the most beautiful girl in Egypt Pike. Elvira and Enos went together like peanut butter and jelly—at least until one fateful day when a man named Broughton made Elvira's acquaintance.

Eager to have the perfect wedding, Enos spent years working long hours and denying himself the pleasures his money could buy. As the day approached, Enos could hardly sit still; his happiness was infectious, and all those who passed the love-struck man on the street couldn't resist returning his goofy grin. It was all anyone could talk about in Egypt Pike. Everyone who could help out in the preparation of the wedding did. Clothes were sewn, dresses hemmed and altered, tablecloths decorated and flowers arranged and collected. So it was little wonder that when Enos and Elvira decided to attend a church picnic, locals were naturally curious as to why Elvira had spent so much of her afternoon in the company not of Enos, but of a tall and handsome stranger who introduced himself simply as Broughton.

Enos dismissed his friends' concerns. He reassured them that there was nothing to worry about, that Elvira could not possibly be interested in the stranger; after all, she had pledged her love to Enos. Some of his friends believed him; others were not quite as convinced. With increasing frequency, Elvira was seen about town accompanied by Broughton. To the objective eye, Elvira's affections had clearly turned to another. But Enos saw none of this. He clung to her pledge of love tightly, holding it to his heart like a security blanket.

Needless to say, Elvira had fallen in love with Broughton. Fearing the town's judgment and wrath, Elvira fled town upon accepting Broughton's proposal. Enos refused to believe the truth, accepting it only when he learned from Elvira's parents that she had, in fact, eloped. She left behind a note and one severely broken heart.

Devastated, Enos couldn't face Egypt Pike. Everyone in his generation and the next would hear about how poor Enos was betrayed and left to writhe in the dust. To face his friends and family, to see the sympathy and sorrow in their eyes, would have been a constant reminder of his loss. If he had reflected more on his next decision, Enos' life might have taken a different turn. As it happened, Enos went to Timmons Bridge with a good length of rope and hanged himself from the rafters of the covered bridge. Other accounts say he wandered into the fields around Egypt Pike and shot himself. In either case, Enos killed himself. Before doing so, though, he was heard uttering, "I'll kill myself and haunt fool lovers till Judgment Day." Enos was through with love and its illusions.

Unlike the treacherous Elvira, the jilted lover was true to his word. As lovers in their buggies made their way across Timmons Bridge, they began experiencing unexplained disturbances. The buggies would rock inexplicably from one side to the other or the doors would mysteriously open, at which point Enos would poke his ghostly head through the opening to leer at the terrified couple inside. As technology evolved, Enos learned to adapt. Even today, people claim that couples might experience some sort of misfortune as they cross Timmons Bridge in their cars. The car may break down, weird voices may arise out of nowhere and boisterous sounds may seem to herald the collapse of the bridge.

Interestingly enough, Enos is careful about who he haunts. Quarreling couples are left alone, as are solitary motorists; only happy couples fear Enos. Because they remind Enos of his tortured and painful past, they draw his ire.

Rogues' Hollow

Miners were a hardy lot. Working long hours in the pitch black of the mines, they were forced to endure torturous working conditions for little pay. For the most part, their labors only added to the wealth of their employers. Their only outlet for venting their frustrations or any grievances they might have had was the saloon—a warm place to exchange their hard-earned dollars for mind-numbing intoxicants. Saloons, naturally, prospered, and enterprising owners flocked to the mining areas, eager to capitalize on this particularly spirited and prosperous trade. What the atmosphere attracted was the hardiest and the leanest of men. In turn, they contributed to the growth of a brutish culture where respect was earned, not given, and where a poorly considered word might be one's last. An outsider had to be careful; he needed a fast tongue and even faster fists.

Just south of Cleveland, in northeast Ohio, there once existed such a place. With more than 100 mines in the area, Rogues' Hollow flourished in the days following the Civil War. It quickly acquired a reputation as being one of the toughest spots in the entire United States, a notoriety built upon the backs of miners who spent their free time and money in one or more of the seven saloons dotting the Hollow. It wasn't a reputation that the people of the Hollow worked hard to discredit. But the coal mines, which established the area as one of the more important coal producers in Ohio, couldn't possibly fuel the local economy forever. By the 1940s, the mines were barren and Rogues' Hollow—which once inspired dread in travelers—shriveled and faded, leaving behind crumbling mineshafts and shanties.

Yet, even now, years after it boomed as a mining town, Rogues' Hollow continues to loom large within the imagination. The miners who once populated the area have left their own monuments—scattered accounts in the form of stories and legends from an area still rich in folklore. An article from the November 1980 issue of *Ohio Magazine* describes the hollow of Rogues' Hollow as a mysterious swath of land, a mile long and an eighth of a mile wide, near Doylestown in Wayne County. A thick canopy of forest and vegetation prevents natural light from reaching the ground below. What little light does reach the undergrowth reflects eerily off the heavy mist on the vegetation, creating a ghostly glow. While the living may have abandoned the place, the spirits apparently have not.

Energy permeates the hollow, a place where the land has allegedly absorbed the combined energies and emotions of past events. While this statement may sound questionable, in a sense it is true. A number of the haunting stories surrounding the hollow have been culled from accounts inevitably revolving around haunted mines, ghost miners and various dancing picks and shovels. One of the more common stories recounts the tragic death of a young miller's assistant. While working one day at William Chidester's wool mill, the young man slipped and fell into a water wheel that crushed him. In spite of his death, the miller's assistant continued to appear for years after, always returning at the same time of day to carry out his chores. Even after the mill had fallen into disuse and had been razed to the ground, the same young man would return. And then an inexplicable fire burnt down the Chidester home in the late 1940s, just days after it had been bought by a Barberton man. Some in town believed that Chidester's young assistant was responsible, disapproving fiercely of the man who had moved into the home. Apparently, the spirit would rather destroy the home than have someone he considered unwelcome live there. A malevolent being? Perhaps, but not nearly as frightening as the one encountered by Mickey Walsh while riding home one night.

The son of a former saloonkeeper, Walsh found the stories about the Ghost Oak Tree amusing. It was said a horse once ran head-first into a frozen bough on the tree; the impact of the crash was enough to sever the hapless horse's head and give rise to the ghost of the headless horse. Walsh thought the accounts would provide some entertainment on a stormy night as he drove his horse team past the Ghost Oak Tree. Even before the team had reached the tree, it came to an abrupt stop. Although Walsh repeatedly lashed his mules, they refused to move. Throwing his hands up, Walsh looked up to the skies for an explanation and saw a sight that caused his blood to run cold. According to Walsh and reports in *Ohio Magazine,* he saw "the Devil himself sitting on the low overhanging bough. His eyes were gleaming like balls of fire."

Walsh claims he fell into a sort of trance and when he finally awoke, his mules were still standing still but the apparition had vanished. He turned his team around and returned home. He would return again, but this time accompanied by a group of his friends. All of them saw the creature again, this time astride the headless horse, peering through them with the same fiery eyes. The apparition rode off, disappearing into a cloud of dust, leaving confused and frightened men in its wake. Since that time, others have reportedly witnessed the same disturbing sight at the Ghost Oak Tree, just another one of the many spirits that still inhabits the long-abandoned Rogues' Hollow.

Johnny Appleseed

John Chapman was born in Leominster, Massachusetts, in 1774. He was a small, wiry man possessed of a seemingly limitless reserve of energy. His hair was dark and long, and to look into his eyes was to peer into the soul of a man of rare wit and brilliance. Since possessions meant little to John, he was often seen wearing cast-off clothing; in his later years, people reported seeing him wearing a burlap sack with holes for his head and arms. He rarely wore shoes, preferring to feel the grass between his toes. All John needed was the company of men, the land and, most importantly, his faith.

John eventually ended up in Pennsylvania, where he imparted a unique gift to families migrating west. He either sold or gave them saplings and apple seeds to plant along the way. In 1801, at 27, John entered the Ohio Territory, weighed down on either side by sturdy, weather-worn leather bags, filled to the brims with seeds. For the rest of his life, John traveled through the Midwest, planting seeds where he found clearings along the bank of a stream. He passed from settlement to settlement, the eternal guest and traveler. And while he never stayed anywhere for more than an evening, his visits were remembered for years. John's gentleness and simplicity appealed to people of all ages, but especially to children, who adored his singing and preaching.

Even Native Americans welcomed John; he stood in contrast to the settlers who encroached upon ancestral lands and plundered the natural wealth of the earth. John was also a great medicine man who wandered freely through territory that most settlers were determined to avoid. Allegedly, during the War of 1812, the ease with which he moved through hostile territory allowed him to travel 30 miles to summon

IN MEMORY OF
JOHN CHAPMAN
FAMOUS "JOHNNY APPLESEED"
BORN IN LEOMINSTER, MASS.
SEPT. 26, 1774
DIED IN FORT WAYNE, IND.
MARCH 18, 1845

WITHOUT A HOPE OF RECOMPENSE,
WITHOUT A THOUGHT OF PRIDE,
JOHN CHAPMAN PLANTED APPLE TREES
AND PREACHED, AND LIVED AND DIED.

The ghost of Johnny Appleseed has been spotted near this monument in Dexter City.

troops to Mansfield, Ohio. This quelled a raid by Indian tribes allied with the British. The rest of his time was spent traveling the Midwest to gather seeds, plant trees and visit his forest nurseries where he would care for his apple trees. The strange man with the pasteboard hat soon became known as Johnny Appleseed.

John died near Fort Wayne, Indiana, in 1845 at the age of 70. But his legend and his ghost live on. People have reported seeing his spirit in two locations: at the Appleseed Monument on Highway 21 in southeastern Ohio, first erected in September 1942; and at his family's cemetery in Dexter City, Noble County. The ghost of the barefoot icon wears a tattered and ratty pair of pants held up by one suspender strap. Still considered one of Ohio's most famous spirits, Johnny Appleseed continues to roam the land today as he did during his life.

7
Captive Spirits

Nobody ever said fate was kind. For prisoners, orphans and the insane, fate can be especially cruel. We might expect that after serving full sentences on earth, captives would transcend this corporeal plane and find altogether different existences elsewhere. But that is often not the case. Prisons are notorious for being haunted; Ohio's institutions are no exception. There are plenty of examples in which captive spirits continue to roam the halls and cells in which they spent many miserable years. Although most of the institutions in this chapter have long been closed, for a select number of spirits they are still quite operational.

Johnson's Island

In 1861, Secretary of War Simon Cameron assigned Lieutenant Colonel William Hoffman the task of managing the new federal prison system. As Commissary General of Prisoners, Hoffman became desperate to find a site on which to build a prison. The Civil War was not going to end anytime soon, and the building would have to house the thousands of Confederate soldiers the Union expected to capture. The site would have to be remote, making escape from the prison all the more difficult. Finally, access to and from the prison would have to be controlled by the federal government.

With these ideas in mind, Hoffman arrived in Sandusky along the northern Ohio shoreline in October 1861. He inspected several islands in Lake Erie aboard the *Island Queen*. After rejecting a number of alternatives, Hoffman chose Johnson's Island.

Three miles north of Sandusky, Johnson's Island was far from the Canadian border and known for its harsh weather. Winter conditions along the Erie shore would prove overwhelming to Confederate prisoners accustomed to warmer and sunnier conditions. The island's size and resources appealed to Hoffman as well. At 300 acres, it was heavily wooded, thick with stands of hickory and oak. When needed, these trees would provide a plentiful fuel source; all other supplies could be obtained from the nearby mainland. Forty acres had already been cleared and the site appeared well-suited for construction, which was put in the hands of two Sandusky builders.

On April 11, 1862, the *Island Queen* ferried the first of the prisoners, 200 in total, to Johnson's Island. A 15-foot high wooden fence ensured that the prisoners stayed inside.

While incarcerated on Johnson's Island, prisoners of war contended with cruel guards, unforgiving cold and little likelihood of escape.

Behind each block stood a sink or privy—a foul-smelling place where waste didn't necessarily drain over the ground's limestone shelf. Each block also had a kitchen at one end with a cast iron stove. The menu was rather limited, ranging from salt fish to pickled beef in a rice and bean stew.

Escape would have been difficult. Anchored just offshore was the gunboat *Michigan*, her guns aimed at the prison walls to break the spirit of any prisoner hoping to escape. Anyone attempting to flee north to Canada faced an arduous 30-mile swim across the forbidding waters of Lake Erie in the summer and a frozen trek in winter. Those hoping to dig through the latrines and out beyond the stockade walls found their way barred by thick, dense layers of limestone. Others, who dared to venture across the frozen lake, found that the comforts of the prison, while small, were sorely missed.

Life on Johnson's Island was difficult. The prison's first warden, William S. Pierson of Sandusky, was replaced because of his incompetence and cruelty towards prisoners of war. The guards, no less, demoralized the inmates by restricting rations, damaging goods sent through the mail and by preventing the Confederates from feeling anything even remotely resembling freedom. There was little the men could do about the weather, disease and the combined pressures of war and captivity.

The gaps in the block walls, for instance, allowed icy blasts of winter's breath to waft in during the winter. Prisoners were forced to stuff newspapers and whatever materials they could find into the cracks for insulation. Pneumonia and fever became constant companions of those weakened by the frigid air. It's alleged that close to 300 prisoners died while at Johnson's Island. All were buried in a small cemetery on the north end of the island.

Johnson's Island was in operation as a prison for almost four years. During that time, more than 10,000 officers and 1000 enlisted men were imprisoned there. When the war ended, prisoners were finally released and sent home—except of course those who stayed behind in the cemetery. While surviving prisoners were treated to warm homecomings, the dead had their wooden grave headboards replaced with Georgia marble. To this day, though, it seems that the dead continue to protest against their harsh treatment while alive.

Early in 20th century, some laborers in Sandusky Bay were quarrying stone. Weather can change quickly in the area in the fall, and where there had just been clear blue skies, there were now big, black rolling clouds. The air cracked and

Workers once saw a ghostly battalion of Confederate captives march out of the prison cemetery.

split with the rumbling of thunder as lightning flashed. Exposed to the elements, the laborers ran for the closest shelter—the wooded groves of the Johnson's Island cemetery. There, huddled beneath the branches, the men saw something spectacular. Amid an eerie green light, figures rose from the graves, coming together to form a company of Confederate soldiers. As the workers would later report, the ghostly soldiers fell into formation and began a march home across the bay.

More recently, visitors have experienced an overwhelming sense of dread as they walk the cemetery grounds. Others have heard the very faint strains of "Dixie," the anthem of the Confederacy, floating softly upon the air. The war may be over, but the echoes of the past continue to ring.

The Athens Lunatic Asylum

In the late 19th and early 20th centuries, mental illness was wildly misunderstood. Those who suffered from its ravages were stigmatized and portrayed as agents of the devil. Physicians entrusted with their care understood little about the diseases they were trying to treat, and in many cases acted on the basis of conjecture and misguided assumptions. The insane were placed in asylums where they were subjected to a variety of physical and mental abuse, ranging from the use of straightjackets and iron restraints to prolonged isolation and humiliation. Drugs such as chloroform, bromides and ether subdued patients who resisted their physical and mental containment. Tainted by fear and prejudice, mental institutions were avoided and shunned. It's not surprising, then, that some mysteries from early American asylums remain unsolved, especially in ones with dark pasts.

Despite the best efforts of social reformers such as Dorothea Dix and Thomas Kirkbride, conditions remained horrific in most institutions. Kirkbride promoted a particular style of asylum, with a quiet countryside setting and attractive grounds to make the institution acceptable to the community. Within the buildings, patients would receive the most comfortable custodial care. Kirkbride recommended that a maximum of 250 patients be housed in an institution.

The Athens Lunatic Asylum was constructed with his model in mind.

The state-of-the-art institution was partially financed by Henry O'Bleness. The building was designed by architect Levi T. Schofield of Cleveland to be a grand representation of the High Victorian or Second Empire style. When completed on New Year's Day 1874, it measured 853 feet in length, 4072 feet around, was four stories high and had 15-foot ceilings. The goal was to provide 577 patients with ample light, space and air. Herman Haerlin of Cincinnati, a disciple of Frederick Law Olmstead, the man behind New York's Central Park, transformed the asylum grounds into a veritable paradise on earth. At the time, the prevailing notion was that anyone unfortunate enough to be admitted to an asylum was there for life; therefore, the grounds had to be stunning. But while the building and the land were designed with an eye towards better patient care, shifting attitudes towards the mentally infirm created an environment that was less than ideal.

Opened on January 9, 1874, the building quickly gained a miserable reputation, partly because many of those deemed insane were actually notorious criminals. One infamous patient was Billy Milligan, one of the first people ever to be acquitted of a crime on the grounds of insanity. Apparently, he had 24 personalities, many of which were violent and murderous. The institution's staff were no angels, either. Accounts of beatings and torture by custodians and doctors accompanied a general disregard for human life. Death and murder were common within this building's walls, creating an uneasy harmony with the institution's bucolic setting on a hill overlooking the Hocking River. Not until Clifford Beers published his book, *A Mind That Found Itself*, did serious reforms begin.

In 1900, Beers was committed to a Connecticut mental institution after suffering a nervous breakdown. The death of his brother had occasioned a failed suicide attempt. He spent eight years at the mercy of incompetent attendants who abused rather than treated him. After his release, he wrote about his experiences, and his book thrust the issue of mental health reform onto the national agenda. Although the resulting changes in public attitudes prompted some improvements in Athens, the institution did not easily shed its tarnished reputation.

By the 1930s, over 1600 patients called the asylum home; by 1953, 1749 were under its care. The escalating population was attributed to scant admittance criteria. Epileptics, menopausal women, alcoholics and tuberculosis victims were all committed, along with seasonal patients who would otherwise be homeless. These patients exacerbated existing problems. At times, one attendant would be responsible for 40 to 50 patients. For those requiring more intensive care, there was one attendant for every 12. The institution came to consist of 78 buildings with land totaling over 1000 acres. It's not unreasonable to assume that patient care suffered during these overcrowded times.

In the 1980s, President Reagan began closing institutions down all over the state. The Athens Mental Health Center was one of them. Newer, stricter definitions of what qualified as mental illness introduced a displaced class of former patients into the social fabric of Athens. Stigmatized and ignored, these vagrants drifted aimlessly, unable to find gainful employment. According to some reports, they still make up a significant portion of Athens' relatively large homeless population.

Interestingly enough, the eeriest chapter in the Athens Mental Health Center's history was written after the building closed. In 1979, Ohio University's student paper, *The Post*, ran a story asking for help in locating a missing patient, a woman who had disappeared from the hospital grounds. It was the policy at the time that patients in open wards could leave the grounds. A strict curfew was enforced: 8 PM in the summer and 6 PM in the winter. The woman had signed out but had never signed back in. A search of the building turned up nothing; in desperation, the center turned to the paper. A search party was organized, but as before, they found no trace of the woman. She had, for all intents and purposes, vanished into thin air.

Days passed, the hospital closed and people lost interest in the missing patient. She faded quickly from the public eye, only to return weeks later in a way no one could have anticipated.

A few weeks after the building had closed, Clarence Allison, a maintenance man, was doing some work in Ward N.20. As he opened the door to the top floor of the three-story ward, he caught sight of something in the shadows. There was also a rotten smell in the air, but stronger and more pungent than anything he'd smelled before. He approached the form slowly and finally peered down to see better. Judging from its smell and the appearance, the body had been there for quite some time. Clarence called the authorities, who identified the body as that of Margaret Schilling. The coroner who performed the autopsy determined that she had died of heart failure and had been dead for at least four to five weeks. Nobody will know for certain why Margaret died in that ward, but the prominent theory is that she somehow stumbled onto the floor. The ward had once been used to treat seriously infected patients, but by the time Margaret made her way there, it was only used for storage.

Custodians and attendants looking for Margaret had searched the ward when she first went missing, but she obviously had hidden. Unfortunately, when the searchers left the floor, they locked its entrance from the outside. She was trapped.

As the days passed, she must have realized that she would die in the institution. She stripped off all her clothes and folded them neatly on the windowsill. Lying down on the concrete floor, she crossed her arms and quietly expired beneath the tall windows.

Her body was removed from the third floor. Underneath, there was a perfect outline of her body imprinted upon the marble floor; looking closely, people could see that the outline had preserved every last detail of Margaret, from the fold and wrinkles of her skin to the style of her hair. The stain was cleaned, but it reappeared again and again. Even to this day, the stain can be seen on the marble floor. Maintenance workers now feel that scrubbing only darkens the stain and that it will fade in time. It's been speculated that the woman's body composition reacted to the steady stream of sunlight that beat down upon her dead body for five weeks and created the imprint.

After the institution closed, most of the buildings and structures of the former Athens Mental Health Center became part of Ohio University. The buildings were opened to the public and guided tours were offered. A highlight of the tour, the stain on the marble floor remains a lingering symbol of the insane asylum's dark history.

Gore Orphanage Road

In many ghost stories, fact and fiction blur into one indistinguishable mass. Such is the case with the stories and legends surrounding Gore Orphanage Road. Although very little can be said with certainty about the unusual accounts of death and haunting, they still fascinate the people living in and around Vermilion.

"Gore Orphanage" sounds like a wonderfully creepy combination of innocence and mayhem, but it couldn't be further from the truth. Gore here doesn't mean blood; instead, it refers to a triangular piece of land created during errors in early surveys of the land. And while the story does involve an orphanage, the institution in question was known as the Orphanage of Light and Hope, a rather optimistic and buoyant name, and especially ironic given the fate of the institution.

Information graciously provided by the Sandusky Follet House Museum Archives has it that one of its many buildings was consumed in a fiery blaze, taking 60 young lives along with it. The area is now reputedly haunted by the souls of these hapless youngsters, with reports from students at nearby Firelands College describing drops of blood materializing out of nowhere on beds of freshly fallen snow, accompanied by a strong smell of decay in the air. Cars parked close to the site find the marks of tiny fingerprints from unseen figures in their frosted-up windows. And near the Vermilion River, it is said that 60 tiny gravestones will light up the night sky as luminescent memorials to the lives allegedly taken in the fire. These are the accounts—the murmurs and whispers. The reality of the situation is something else entirely.

The history of the Orphanage of Light and Hope begins in 1902. The Sprungers, newly arrived from Bern, Indiana, decided to open a home for children, spurred to help those unable to help themselves by the deaths of their own children. They settled near Vermilion and bought up land and farms in the area known as Swift's Hollow. It was their dream to create their own little utopia, a place where they could remain independent of the whims of others. Even though they were devout, God-fearing individuals, they refused the sponsorship offered by a church association. They wanted to create a self-sustaining orphanage that occasionally relied on the good patronage of those willing to donate either time or money. Most of the time, they planned to live off the land. From their original plots of land in Swift's Hollow, they acquired more farms and farmland, buying up property from John Hughes and Joseph Howard. Their holdings came to comprise more then 500 acres of land, on which they grew their own food and sustenance for 70 milk cows, 100 hogs, 100 head of sheep and a large flock of poultry. A huge silo was erected, as was a milk house, a chapel room and a small printing press. The children would assist with the farm work and housekeeping, and they would raise enough money from livestock and poultry.

Children between 2 and 12 would be admitted regardless of creed or nationality, and they would be supported until 20. During their time in the Orphanage of Light and Hope, they would form and learn a trade. Boys would live at the Hughes farm, girls at the Howard farm. The Sprungers had enough room to accommodate 120 children, and, in 1906, they added a nursery to receive babies who were only a few weeks old.

Unfortunately, despite the best of intentions, the Sprungers' decision not to take on any formal financial backing would prove to be a costly mistake. In 1914, Mr. Sprunger, who had invested heavily in the project, became fatally ill and died, leaving the running of the orphanage to his wife. She inherited an organization that was far from efficient and profitable. Walter Malone of the Friends' Church of Cleveland eventually took over as superintendent, but no amount of experience or managerial skills could overcome the sobering fact that Light and Hope simply wasn't making enough to support farm labor or school teachers. Since the orphanage was indebted to a Vermilion bank and was unable to make payments, the bank foreclosed on the mortgage in 1916 and the buildings were vacated. The children were dispersed throughout Cleveland to various families. The tract of land on which the orphanage stood was eventually sold to another party.

One of the buildings eventually burned down, but no one can seem to agree as to when. Some accounts claim it was in 1912, when the orphanage would have still been in operation; others say it was in 1920. Regardless of when the accident happened, there were no reported casualties, lending no credence to the story that an evil administrator had locked 60 children in the barn and then torched the place—the legend that undoubtedly gave rise to rumors that circulated through the Firelands College student body. So how did the Orphanage of Light and Hope become tied to the story of death and terror? It seems that two separate stories were conflated.

Near the orphanage, in Swift's Hollow, was a magnificent structure, a one-story home with 14 bedrooms, six fireplaces, servants' quarters and a magnificent veranda with large Greek pillars. Built in 1841 at a cost of $15,000, the home became known as the Swift Home. When, in 1865, the owner was rendered insolvent by a combination of poor investment speculations and defaulted loans, he sold the house and moved to Michigan where he died in 1878.

The Swift Home was sold to a group of spiritualists, a sect of people who believed that when one's corporeal form dies, the soul continues to exist and can communicate with the living through a medium. Tragedy struck this family in the winter of 1893, when four children in the home died of diphtheria. According to local lore, the children were never really dead, as their spirits could be contacted through séances. Soon enough, there were whispers that the dead children were haunting the Swift Home—perhaps, some thought, there was something to the spiritualist doctrine after all. Then, in 1923, long after the home had been abandoned and fallen into disrepair, the place was consumed in a fiery blaze.

Over time, the two separate stories merged into one, and soon enough the orphanage was said to be haunted by the souls of not four, but 60 children. Today, there are still those who believe in the story. What was once the orphanage plot is now a desolate stretch of land, 150 feet down a ravine along the Vermilion River. The voices heard there come not from the dead, but from the groups of teenagers who flock to the area to drink, smoke and to do whatever else suits them. Some claim it is a dangerous area, not because of spirits rising, but because of spirits ingested. In 2000, 500 reported incidents led safety officials and residents to propose the temporary closure of Gore Orphanage Road. Lorain County officials found their hands tied and had no authority to close the roadway. The parties in the ravine often turn violent, and while the Orphanage of Light and Hope closed years ago, it would appear that the area in which it once stood is still a home, of sorts, for children. Sadly, though, the optimistic vision in which the Sprungers placed so much of their faith has given way to the rebelliousness of misled youth.

The Old Mansfield Reformatory

At one time, the grounds in Mansfield were home to more than 4000 soldiers training for combat in the Civil War. When the camp opened in 1861, it was known as Camp Mordecai Bartley, named for a former governor of Ohio. By the late 1880s, attention in Mansfield had shifted from armed conflict to corrections.

When the first cornerstone for an intermediate state prison was laid on the former site of Camp Mordecai Bartley, newspapers called the event "Mansfield's Greatest Day." An estimated 15,000 people gathered to witness the ceremony, and included dignitaries such as Senator John Sherman, Governor J.B. Foraker, General Roeliff Brinkerhoff and former president Rutherford B. Hayes. Construction involved the combined efforts of both business and political leaders who wanted the prison brought to Mansfield—a campaign that had begun shortly after the Civil War. Finally, in 1884, the state legislature allowed for the creation of an intermediate penitentiary to fill the gap between the Boys' Industrial School in Lancaster and the Ohio Penitentiary in Columbus. A board appointed by the governor was swayed enough by the enthusiasm of the Mansfield contingent to select Mansfield as the site for the Ohio State Reformatory.

Mansfield began a whirlwind of fundraising, eager to collect enough money to buy land for the reformatory. The building design, by Cleveland architect Levi T. Scofield, was allegedly modeled on sketches of Old World German castles. There were problems securing the necessary funds, and it took a decade before the Ohio State Reformatory was finally able to accept its first group of inmates. When the new prison was officially opened, 150 inmates were transferred from the Ohio Penitentiary. According to news reports at the time, the arrival of the inmates was subject to much celebration. Crowds thronged the train tracks outside the reformatory to watch the prisoners being unloaded and admitted.

While the prison was initially regarded as a model for others to emulate, its reputation quickly disintegrated. As early as 1933, the Ohio State Reformatory drew fire for its overcrowded conditions. A group of educators and penologists conducting research found the living conditions disgraceful; they were careful to note that the overcrowded conditions led to a majority rule and little rehabilitative value. In the 1970s, it was suggested that the reformatory be torn down and replaced by a network of smaller institutions, each housing no more than 500 inmates. And in 1978, with public outrage reaching a fever pitch, the Counsel for Human Dignity filed a federal lawsuit on behalf of the 2200 inmates of the prison, claiming that their living conditions denied them basic rights as human beings. The lawsuit was finally settled five years later with an agreement stipulating that prison conditions would be improved and the cell blocks would be closed by the end of 1986. It wasn't until 1990 that the last of the staff and inmates were finally moved from the Ohio State Reformatory.

In 1994, the outbuildings, surrounding wall and power plant were demolished. A year later, Ohio leased the land to the city of Mansfield, which, in turn, leased it to the Mansfield Reformatory Preservation Society—a move that allowed the building to celebrate its centennial in October 1996. Tours are now conducted through the old building, and its fame has spread through exposure in films such

Deaths, mysterious and otherwise, have left a powerful paranormal impression at the Mansfield Reformatory.

as *Air Force One* and *The Shawshank Redemption*. At six floors, its east cell block is the world's largest free-standing cell block. But while the prison is no longer occupied by living inmates, some swear that the halls and cells of what is now the Mansfield Reformatory are still home to the spirits of some of the thousands of individuals who were interred there. Life inside the reformatory, after all, was often precarious.

Accounts of tragedies and deaths abound. Some individuals condemned to solitary confinement found the isolation simply too much to bear. Unable to deal with the company of their own personal demons, some managed to hang themselves, while others engaged in self-immolation, setting themselves on fire with lighter fluid or paint thinner. A riot in 1957 caused 120 prisoners to serve 30-day terms in solitary confinement; but with only 20 cells down in "the Hole," two inmates at a time were forced to occupy the same cell, giving overcrowding a whole new meaning. In one instance, only one inmate walked out. The other had been killed, his body stuffed like an extra bedroll under the cell bunk. Even those charged with the supervision of the prisoners were not immune to tragedy.

In the 1950s, an accident, still shrouded in mystery to this day, occurred in the warden's living quarters. The warden and his wife were not on the best of terms. One unfortunate day, as the wife was pulling down a jewelry box from a closet shelf, she knocked a gun down from its perch and it misfired. The bullet lodged itself in her left lung and she died. While her death was ruled accidental, some claimed that it was a murder cleverly orchestrated by her husband. One theory posits that a divorce would have been frowned upon, especially for a man in the warden's position. Another, related by Nick Reiter and Lori Schillig of the Avalon Foundation, also proposes that marital strife was the motivating factor, but it was related to the warden's illicit affair with the house boy. Interestingly enough, the boy was paroled following the incident. Nine years later, the warden, while working at his desk, suffered a heart attack and died. The wardens who followed refused to live in the quarters, choosing instead to keep their families off the prison grounds.

Two corrections officers were also killed while at the Ohio State Reformatory. The first died in 1926 when a paroled inmate, Philip Orleck, returned to the prison to aid in the escape of a friend; the plan was thwarted when a 72-year-old guard, Urban Wilford, stumbled upon Orleck. Wilford was promptly shot for his troubles, and he died just outside the west gate. Orleck was arrested two months later and eventually died in the electric chair. The other guard, Frank Hanger, was beaten to death with an iron bar as a dozen prisoners attempted to flee in 1932.

With all the death and misfortune, it's not surprising that the prison has become the subject of much speculation. It seems like the perfect home for the spirits of the long dead. The rumors of ghosts and hauntings attract ghost hunters to the reformatory from all over the country, all eager to prove for certain whether or not the old prison is haunted. If it is, who exactly is still imprisoned within the reformatory's walls?

On two separate occasions, Reiter and Schillig journeyed to the Mansfield Reformatory to see what they could discover. They knew its reputation for being haunted, but intentionally denied themselves any more information. They wanted to avoid having their perceptions influenced or swayed by any of the stories. Once there, they were guided through the prison while they recorded data with cameras, EVP tape recordings and by room-to-room dowsing, a method akin to divining for water. Reiter was charged with operating the instruments, while Schillig took care of the dowsing. She also made sure to perform psychometric sweeps of the rooms, feeling for impressions or images of an object's history by touching or examining it.

One of the reformatory's walls was decorated and used in the Hollywood blockbuster Air Force One.

By day's end, the two had toured through the guard tower, the chapel and the administrative wings. Strange events happened throughout the day, with equipment malfunctioning for no apparent reason, only to repair itself later. When Reiter returned to the chapel to collect his tape recorder, he found, to his consternation, that nothing had been recorded; mysteriously, the recorder had been paused. While Reiter allowed that he might have accidentally pushed the PAUSE button himself, he "is usually quite careful about such things." When he turned the recorder on again, he made sure it was indeed recording. Later, when the tape was played back, the two heard what was described as a "tapping sound, not unlike a fingernail tapping on the recorder itself."

During the course of her psychometric sweeps, Schillig sensed, on more than one occasion, different essences and feelings, but never more strongly than when she entered the east administrative wing, which once housed the warden's living quarters. Inside its old pink tiled bathroom, Schillig and Reiter both felt extremely eerie and awful sensations, some so powerful that Schillig was rendered nauseous. In another room, Schillig felt the presence of a woman; it wasn't until she had left the room that she learned the room had once been the warden's wife's bedroom. Was it the spirit of the woman who died in an accidental shooting that Schillig sensed?

When their photographs from the trip were developed, they found that several of them contained orbs. After ruling out the ones that might have been caused by reflections of dust particles in front of the lens, there were still seven photos in which orbs could be seen. When asked about their meaning, Reiter said, "No one knows. They may be some concentrated form of energy, like ball lightning except very low powered. They may represent spirits, or they may merely be an unusual form of energy."

Orbs represent the unexplained and may stand as testament to the presence of something otherworldly. That five of the seven photographs were from the administrative wings is consistent with the belief that the dead wife haunts the reformatory, still seeking to uncover the truth behind her untimely death.

When Reiter and Schillig returned to the reformatory months later, they continued to find that their photographs